Superhero Movies

ΙΙ0658988

www.pocketessentials.com

Superhero Movies

Liam Burke

www.pocketessentials.com

First published in 2008 by Pocket Essentials,
P. O. Box 394, Harpenden, Herts, AL5 1JX
www.pocketessentials.com
© Liam Burke, 2008

A CIP catalogue record for this book is available from the British Library.

ISBN 13: 978-1-84243-275-4

2 4 6 8 10 9 7 5 3 1

Typeset by Avocet Typeset, Chilton, Aylesbury, Bucks
Printed and bound in Great Britain by CPI Cox & Wyman, Reading, RG1 8EX

Acknowledgements

I would like to thank the following people for helping to get this book off the ground: Graph-Man Andrew Rea, the inventor of Kryptopedia Gar O'Brien, my family for their unwavering support, and of course the legendary Stan Lee for his gracious contribution, giving this book its extra POW!

Dedicated to my Lois Lane, Helen; who now knows more about superheroes than any right-thinking person should.

Contents

In a Single Bound? Superheroes on Screen

Following a flurry of whizzing blue lights, the camera pans down from the stars to a lonely crystalline planet. Moving closer, a solitary dome is revealed amidst a cityscape built from large shards of glass. Inside, a stodgy-looking Marlon Brando, dotted with sequins, is passing judgement on an irate Terence Stamp. Not long after, this barren planet Krypton explodes; its sole survivor, an infant destined for Earth.

So opens Richard Donner's 1978 film *Superman*, and with it the modern age of superhero movies. Recently, Superman returned to find he was not the only superhero flying the cinematic skies. Among the Man of Steel's many rivals include his DC Comics stablemate Batman, who, after detoxing from an overdose of mid-1990s camp, has returned to his cape and cowl career with renewed vigour and purpose. A number of young turks have also been tugging at Superman's cape, the most eager being the arachnid-themed *wunderkind* Spider-Man, who not only adopted Superman's red-and-blue style, but seems intent on rivalling the Man of Steel's film output. With blind vigilantes, schools of mutants and the occasional green goliath, the Last Son of Krypton now has a big super-family.

Today it seems that, after decades of struggle, caped wonders are making the leap to the screen in a single bound. But why has this super-surge taken place now, when supermen have been righting wrongs since the pages of *Action Comics # 1* in 1938? These first superheroes helped allay the anxieties of comic-book readers in the lead up to and during World War II, allowing fans to identify with indestructible heroes such as Captain America who socked Hitler in the jaw on the cover of his very first issue – a full year before his country joined the war effort in the wake of Pearl Harbour. Though some of these early comic-book heroes, including Superman, Batman and Captain America, did make their way into radio, television and film serials, none would produce a superhero movie.

In the 1960s, comics again sparked a renewed interest in superheroes with a Marvel Comics-led revival of these masked men. These new marvels, such as Spider-Man, Fantastic Four and X-Men, were high-flying heroes with real-world problems – the perfect foil for the silver screen. Yet only a few enjoyable but campy television series emerged, the most enduring example being the Adam West-starring *Batman*. While West's *Batman* did produce a spin-off feature, it was merely an extension of the series rather than an entity of its own. Filmgoers would have to wait 40 years after the first comics to see a Man of Steel fly, and even this cinematic success only resulted in some increasingly anaemic sequels. In 1989, Tim Burton's *Batman* proved successful in blazing a trail, as other gothic vigilantes (*Darkman*, *The Shadow* and *The Phantom*) subsequently made their way onto the screen. But these damp imitators and the justifiably derided Joel Schumacher-directed Batman sequels were Kryptonite to any respectable superhero's big-screen ambitions.

However, with the dawning of the new millennium, the superhero evolved. Gone were the lycra suits, risible puns and juvenile antics. Superheroes were new men; they were X-Men. In 2000, Bryan Singer's *X-Men*, taking its serious approach from *Superman* and its black-leather style from *Batman*, was a superhero movie for a modern audience. Employing a realistic tone and reverence for its source material, *X-Men* appealed to fans and newcomers alike, which was reflected in its strong box office and glowing critical reception. But the mutants' triumph was not enough to claim the superhero-movie *coup d'état* a success; in the past *Superman* and *Batman* had also shown promise as genre-starters only to later fizzle out. To build on the X-Men's momentum, and to make the superhero movie a cinematic institution, another successful film was needed, and the friendly neighbourhood Spider-Man was more than obliging.

Released in 2002, *Spider-Man* not only echoed *X-Men*'s success but amplified it with a worldwide tally of $821 million. Since the success of *Spider-Man*, superhero movies have begun to go as readily with cinema popcorn as butter and salt; they have become the highlights of summer seasons, spinning off into endless series. These films manage to keep cinema tills ringing by providing some of the best big-screen spectacle since the first time Indiana Jones hung up his bullwhip. More than just popcorn-fodder, series such as *X-Men* and *Spider-Man* have rejuvenated and legitimised 'the blockbuster' after all the Phantom Menaces and world-ending asteroids saw the tradition become synonymous with over-stylised puff pieces; while recent franchise restarts *Batman Begins* and *Superman Returns* look set to continue the trend. So with movie studios and audiences now clearly cured of their fear of flying, the question still remains: why are heroes so super now?

A regularly cited reason for this rise of the superhero movie is the advancement of special effects. But although the contribution of digital technologies is not to be undervalued, with Spider-Man now able to seamlessly swing through pixel-populated environments, this argument fails to consider the science fiction and fantasy genres, equally reliant on special tinkering, thriving since Georges Méliès first took a trip to the Moon in 1902. Furthermore, the lack of digital technologies did not stop Ray Harryhausen from realising Sinbad's seventh voyage, nor did Fritz Lang need an endless stream of ones and zeros to populate his futuristic *Metropolis*. From as far back as the 1950s and the George Reeves-starring *Adventures of Superman* television series, audiences believed a man could fly; recent computer-aided effects have just given him the lift he needed to soar.

A more likely motive for this superhero-movie boom is not the digital ones and zeros that make Superman fly, but rather the number of zeros on the box-office receipts after he's come back down to Earth. Once *X-Men* scored a worldwide gross of nearly

$300 million on a penny-pinching $75 million budget, movie studios began to see the financial incentive in keeping these heroes in subterranean lairs and figure-hugging jumpsuits.

Another probable reason for this super-surge is the lack of imagination endemic in Hollywood moviemaking, a business crippled by a creative cowardice that aims for the lowest common denominator, often resulting in the banal. The overriding practice seems to be, why have one good idea produce only one good film, when you can pillage it for a number of films? Thus audiences get force-fed pointless prequels, needless television remakes and more penguins on screen than on a melting Antarctic glacier. For now, Hollywood will continue to give every character ever to don spandex the cinematic treatment until Plastic Man becomes the subject of a big-budget trilogy. Fortunately, with a 70-year stockpile of stories and characters, superheroes can take this creative mining.

In fact superheroes, with their never-ending crusades for justice, are the gift that keeps on giving. Boy wizards may grow up and trips to Mordor come to an end, but decades after they first slipped on their capes, many superheroes are still flying through the same skies as when they began. These modern-day Sisyphuses' perpetual conflicts are such a renewable source of energy that even Al Gore would have to approve, providing yet another reason for greedy film studios to forage through the pages of the nearest four-colour wonder for inspiration.

Yet cinema audiences are not the mindless demographics Hollywood would wish them to be, and no amount of manufactured hype will dupe filmgoers into paying to see the exploits of a caped crusader unwillingly. Nonetheless, audiences gladly continue to support the ongoing adventures of Superman and Batman while inviting new heroes, not only into their multiplexes but also into their living rooms, where the plainclothes superhumans of *Heroes* now reside. So where does this insatiable appetite for people with omnipotent powers come from?

Superheroes on the comic-book page first came to prominence in the prelude to World War II. That Superman could do the things in comics that people wished they could do in their everyday lives provided an escape for readers during an age fraught with peril. Today, with the events of 9/11 and the subsequent War on Terror, the world again finds itself in uncertain times as constant television images remind us how powerless we can sometimes be. If cinema represents for many the great escape, then, with horrors on our doorstep, the idea of taking that journey with heroes who can turn back time and always save the world seems like a tempting prospect.

Any one of these reasons could explain the recent, unprecedented success of superhero movies, with it more likely being a combination of all those mentioned and a few more not yet considered. Whatever the cause, today superheroes are everywhere; but who are these Men of Tomorrow?

In 2003, the American Film Institute (AFI) selected its 100 greatest movie heroes and villains. Leading the side of the angels was Atticus Finch, a character who wistfully intoned, 'You never know someone until you step inside their skin,' and for the villains, Hannibal 'the Cannibal' Lecter, a man who did just that. Cinema's first superhero, Superman, came in at a respectable 26, Batman scraped into the top 50 at 46 with his arch-nemesis the Joker faring one better at 45 in the villains list, while the likes of Spider-Man and the X-Men failed to make the grade. Though Atticus Finch and Superman share a number of similarities – both fight for Truth, Justice and the American Way while using bespectacled mild manners to hide a hero's resolve – no one is likely to confuse the gallant southern lawyer with the Last Son of Krypton. However, there were many heroes on the AFI list whose feats could be considered 'super': the Terminator is quite literally a Man of Steel, Obi-Wan Kenobi travelled through the stars and Indiana Jones has punched out as many Nazis as Captain America ever did.

So what makes these heroes 'super'? Is it just the snappy dressing and subterranean lairs? The superhero goes beyond, or rather beneath, the hero's mask. Superheroes are the continuation of a mythology that includes Achilles, Samson, Hercules, Robin

Hood and Zorro. From the point at which Superman became the mythological icon of the twentieth century, a distinct superhero archetype was laid down. This broad archetype was quickly fashioned to a strict form by other entrants to the pantheon: Batman, Captain America *et al*. Consequently, one could propose a rigid model to which superheroes conform:

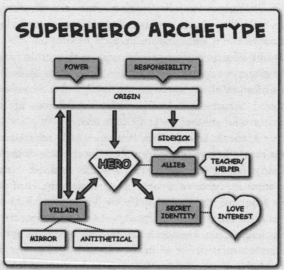

This superhero archetype began with the comic book superheroes and continued into their big-screen adaptations, with newly created cinematic heroes Mr Incredible, RoboCop, and *Unbreakable*'s David Dunn adhering to the formula. There are elements of these archetypal traits in all of cinema's superheroes; but what is this superhero archetype that forms the basis of characters and films as varied as *Superman*, *Hellboy* and *Buffy the Vampire Slayer*?

Examination of this superhero archetype should begin, as these heroes do, with their origins. In superhero movies two events shape the character's origin, which have been clearly identified in the truism Spider-Man follows fastidiously: 'With great power comes great responsibility'. These events are the origin of the 'power' and the origin of the heroic 'responsibility'. The origin of the 'power', or special abilities a hero will use, usually occurs first in the story. Like much of superhero lore, the origin is indicative of the times in which it was created. Thus, the origin of Superman's power can be seen to epitomise the successful American immigrant experience of the early twentieth century, with Kal-El (Superman's Kryptonian name) reinventing himself on US soil where he is openly accepted and cherished, whilst retaining elements of his native cultural identity. By the 1960s, rapid technological advancements meant that, for the first time, man had the ability to travel beyond his planet, or leave it in ruins. The manner by which heroes such as the Fantastic Four, Hulk and Spider-Man gained their powers articulated the growing public anxiety over space travel, nuclear attack and scientific research. America in the 1960s was also marked by the civil rights movement, and this concern too was expressed within the environs of the superhero genre, with the feared and hated X-Men found to represent those oppressed peoples. Furthermore, the enmity between pacifist Professor Xavier, leader of the X-Men, and the militaristic Magneto was seen to reflect the ideological opposition of Dr Martin Luther King and Malcolm X that existed at the time of the comic's creation.

The eventual superhero movies, though faithful to the characters' time-tested origins, have added their own inflections, contemporising antiquated concerns with modern ones. Thus in the film adaptation of 2002, Spider-Man does not gain his powers from a radioactive spider, but rather from one that has been genetically engineered, replacing the lessened danger posed by radioactivity with one of genetic engineering and its potential implications for our future society. Similarly, Bruce Banner no longer becomes the Hulk through exposure to gamma radiation alone; this transformation is now triggered by the reminder of childhood traumas, which unleash the primal monster. This need for the film to validate the Hulk's physical transformation with a psychological motive is indicative of today's more cerebral culture. Also, the X-Men films have used the idea of mutancy and alienation to present an allegory for gay rights. This parallel becomes particularly clear in *X2: X-Men United* when the teen mutant Iceman must 'come out' to his parents as a mutant, to which his mother responds, 'Have you tried not being a mutant?'

The second event that anchors the superhero archetype is the origin of the hero's 'responsibility'. While this may take place concurrent to the origin of the power, it is a distinct, usually tragic, event. In the Spider-Man origin, for example, we see how, upon receiving his powers, Spider-Man does not immediately use his gifts in defence of Truth, Justice and the American Way, but rather to make some money and impress a girl (arguably the real American Way). His cavalier attitude to his gifts sees him allow a criminal, who he could easily have stopped, escape from the scene of a crime. When his uncle is shot and killed by what is later revealed to be the same criminal, Spider-Man learns that 'with great power comes great responsibility', and thus the (super)hero is born. Equally traumatic events have motivated many other heroes' origins. Batman's power comes from years of training and an impressive array of gadgets, but he was set on his heroic quest following the murder of his parents by a lowly criminal. Likewise, Daredevil's powers may stem from his exposure to chemical waste, but his heroic impulse to fight crime comes from his father's murder by mob enforcers.

Much like the origin of the power, the origin of the hero's responsibility has been made more concise and subsequently more intense by its cinematic rendering. Where once these characters garnered their heroic responsibility at the hands of random criminals, the films have modified these criminal identities to that of villains the heroes will confront at the film's climax. Consequently, in *Batman*, Bruce Wayne's parents are not killed by the lowlife Joe Chill as they are in the comics, but rather by a young Joker who the adult Bruce Wayne, as Batman, will later face; Daredevil's father is no longer murdered by average mobsters but the future Kingpin of crime in his formative years; and, in the latest cinematic amendment, the until-now 'lone criminal' who shot Spider-Man's uncle was revealed to have had an accomplice in *Spider-Man 3*: the Sandman, one of the film's villains. These alterations to the superhero origin provide a more symmetrical narrative that cinema audiences have come to expect, as opposed to the perpetual conflicts that mark comic superhero narratives. Like the re-contextualisation of the hero's power, these changes are expected and befit the medium in which the superheroes now find themselves, allowing for a more cyclical superhero archetype.

Once a character takes on the mantle of a hero their identity is split between that of superhero and his secret identity. Secret identities are synonymous with the superhero archetype; for every caped crusader there is a hurried costume change in a phone booth, and with every nocturnal protector there must be an awkward daytime alter-ego. Often these two identities are locked in an antagonistic relationship: Superman struggles to find plausible reasons as to why Clark Kent is never around; rather than scour the city for dates as the playboy Bruce Wayne, Batman would prefer to stalk the night-time cityscape for criminals; and Spider-Man must engage villains with the much more deadly threat of school in the morning hanging over his head. However, no matter how cumbersome the secret identity may seem to the superhero, it is essential to the superhero archetype.

The success of the superhero lies in the contrast with his/her alter-ego. To see this archetypal trait manifest itself in superhero movies, one need only look at the prototypical hero Superman and his alter-ego Clark Kent. Their opposition stems from the contrast between Superman as the confident hero, the indestructible 'Man of Steel', and Clark Kent the clumsy, bookish coward. Thus, Kent's weakness serves to highlight Superman's heroism. Binaries such as Superman/Clark Kent permeate the superhero archetype: Bruce Wayne is a pompous, egotistical dandy while Batman is a dedicated silent avenger; Peter Parker is a shy, gawky teenager whereas Spider-Man is a cocky adventurer; and Bruce Banner is a frail, temperate, scientific genius but his monstrous alternate is the rampaging wall of green muscle known as the Hulk. It is interesting that few superheroes actually perform acts

17

of social betterment when in their alias's guise, with honest lawyer Matt Murdock (Daredevil) being one of the few exceptions. Most live meek, civilian lives that allow them to monitor when their Superhero identities may be needed; both Peter Parker and Clark Kent work for busy city newspapers and Bruce Wayne sits in the safety of his Batcave silently viewing monitors.

The superhero archetype relies on the secret identity, not just to accentuate the hero, but to ensure the hero's image is not beyond the reach of the spectator's self-identification. This aspect of the secret identity has been explored by philosopher and novelist Umberto Eco in respect to Superman. In his essay *The Myth of Superman*, he attests that by the way in which 'Clark Kent appears fearful, timid, awkward, near-sighted and submissive, he personifies fairly typically the average reader [or viewer in the case of superhero movies] who is harassed by complexes and despised by his fellow man'. The hero's all-too-human alter-ego allows for audience identification and is emphasised, even exploited, by superhero movies that wish to appeal to a larger audience than the comics on which they are based.

In superhero movies the protagonist is also supported in his quest by many allies who can generally be classified as teachers and helpers. Teachers include Ra's Al Ghul who trained the young Bruce Wayne in martial arts as seen in *Batman Begins*, while helpers are typified by his butler Alfred and Police Commissioner Gordon who aid the adult Bruce Wayne as Batman in his vendetta against his city's criminal fraternity. Another ally readily associated with superheroes is the sidekick, a young partner who parallels the hero. However, this character type is only found among older characters such as Batman and Captain America, created at a time when simpler plotting did not let the real-world irresponsibility of placing an adolescent in danger impede the story. That the image of a superhero flanked by a sidekick endures is largely due to the continuing influence of the 1960s *Batman* television series, in which the caped crusader never left the Batcave without his trusty ward Robin in tow. The only appearance of a traditional sidekick in a superhero movie would again come from the superhero genre's very own Sherlock Holmes and Watson, Batman and Robin, with the Boy Wonder being added to the late 1990s Batman films *Batman Forever* and *Batman & Robin*. Although another unsuccessful element in a pair of films crippled by poor creative decisions, Robin fulfilled the role of the prototypical sidekick in being an adolescent whose origin and abilities parallel that of the main hero; whose presence could reiterate the hero's origin for late-comers to the franchise; and who by echoing the hero's archetype would become an integral part of it.

Even in the early days of comic books and serials, superheroes had more than just sidekicks for company, with damsels such as Lois Lane and Vicki Vale constantly in distress. Yet, early superheroes seemed to have sublimated their sexual desire beneath a higher calling for justice. But as comics progressed with more complex narratives, and began to be adapted into other media that generally require a romantic element, the tricky issue of sexual desire needed to be negotiated within the fabric of the superhero archetype. While today superhero relationships are as much a part of the character on the page as they are on the screen, in many ways cinema is responsible for the superhero sexual awakening, with Superman, the most virtuous and dedicated of superheroes, found going on a date with Lois Lane in *Superman*, consummating their relationship in *Superman II* and, in *Superman Returns*, even fathering her illegitimate child. Cinema brought sex to superheroes and now cinema is using sex to sell superheroes. Whether it is Spider-Man's swinging-in-the-rain kiss or Daredevil's scantily clad, ninja-assassin girlfriend Elektra, relationships have not only become a central part of the superhero's archetype, but also their movies.

While the hero's relationship with his helpers, teachers and love interests bolsters the superhero archetype, no relationship is more central to defining the superhero than that of the hero and his villain. In many ways a superhero does not exist until the villain attacks, waiting like shadows in their civilian identities for the sound of screeching police sirens or the flicker of a familiar signal in the sky; a superhero without a megalomaniac to stop is just a weirdo in a cape. Also, it seems, the more sinful the villain, the more laudable the superhero – a street thug is ok, but a deranged scientist is better, while stopping a world-threatening evil will make you the flavour of the month around the Hall of Justice. The clothes may make the (super)man, but it is the villain that makes him a hero.

In superhero movies the duality of the hero and villain extend beyond the obvious opposition of good and evil. Two distinct categories of supervillain exist, both of which are locked in an antagonistic relationship with the hero – a relationship that defines them both. The first category is those villains who by their very nature are the antithesis of everything that epitomises the hero; the first entrant to this canon of antithetical villains being Superman's arch-nemesis Lex Luthor. While Superman is deified for compassionately using his otherworldly physical powers, Lex Luthor uses his intellect to indulge his base human emotions of lust and greed, and his brains to combat the hero's brawn. Other antithetical villains in superhero movies include honest lawyer Matt Murdock's arch-nemesis, the criminal Kingpin, and Mr Glass, the fragile villain who the *Unbreakable* David Dunn must ultimately face.

The second category of villain is those who are cut from the same cloth as the hero, often sharing a similar background, but have taken an alternate path that now sets them against the hero. These villains, so like the heroes in all aspects but one, hold up a distorted mirror to the central protagonists, helping define by their contrast the superhero. Among the mirror villains seen in superhero movies are the Spider-Man foes the Green Goblin and Doctor Octopus who both, like Peter Parker, were scientists who took on creature-like identities once given powers by laboratory accidents, but unlike Peter they use their power irresponsibly for their own betterment. An unmistakable example of the mirror villain is Professor Xavier's tainted reflection Magneto. This destiny-entwined pair, who once worked together to help the fledgling mutant race take its first steps in the world, now find that their diverging methods bring them into constant conflict. These villains are the protagonists' darkest shadows, helping to sharpen our view of the hero by their contrast.

The hero/villain duality is so central to the superhero archetype that it would provide the basis of *Unbreakable*, a superhero movie with a hero that was the original creation of writer/director M Night Shyamalan (*The Sixth Sense*). The film is steeped in self-referential superhero rhetoric to the point that when the villain is revealed, he berates the hero and audience for not recognising it earlier, saying, 'It all makes sense; in a comic you know how you can tell who the arch-villain is going to be? He's the exact opposite of the hero.' Superhero movies also intensify this relationship, with the villains becoming more actively involved in the hero's origin than in their comic-book sources. Dialogue such as, 'I made you, you made me first' (*Batman*), 'What they did created me' (*V for Vendetta*) and, 'Now that we know who you are, I know who I am' (*Unbreakable*) is littered throughout superhero movies, highlighting the central importance of this antagonistic relationship to the superhero archetype.

These various facets of the superhero archetype, from the traumatised childhoods to the love/hate hero/villain relationships, reappear across the many vigilantes, mutants, vampire slayers and spandex aficionados who populate the superhero movies. This book will use the archetype to unmask these superheroes and their films. *Superhero Movies* brings together superheroes from all walks of life for the first time: DC old-timers will rub shoulders with Marvel whippersnappers; comic adaptations will sit beside big-screen originals; it doesn't matter whether they are green, blue or animated, if they have ever saved the day they are here.

First, some housekeeping: while Marvel and DC Comics may have copyrighted the term 'Super Hero', not all superheroes come from comic books, with some of the best superhero movies, such as *Unbreakable* and *The Incredibles*, realised straight for the screen. Hence this book, though making reference to the comic books that have inspired them, is about the films first.

The book itself is divided across eight chapters of thematically linked heroes, from *Supermen with Feet of Clay* to *Wonder Women*. Each chapter will focus on the most influential films in that area. One should note that 'influential' does not always mean 'best'; for example *X2: X-Men United* may be, in many people's opinions, the mutants' best cinematic outing, but it was *X-Men* which put the team on screen and ignited the current superhero-movie boom, so the spotlight will therefore be on the first feature. However, completists need not worry: your favourite films will be covered, if not in a 'Focus On' feature then in the introductions to each chapter. Some chapters are larger than others (there being many more vigilantes than superheroines), while an entire chapter has been devoted to the Man of Steel (well, he was here first), but every type of hero is well catered for.

Also, there are certain superhero movies that could fit into a number of chapters and will therefore be included in the chapter where they have the greatest relevance. So while Buffy may be a supernatural, vampire-slaying vigilante who is equally cursed and blessed by her gifts, as one of the few ass-kicking heroines she will be filed under Wonder Women. Importantly, in the 'Focus On' features each verdict is delivered with the benefit of hindsight; though *Batman* may have been the most popular film of 1989, this does not necessarily mean it holds up today. If you disagree with a verdict, dip into your DVD collection and see if it is the same film you remember.

Finally, this book is at its core a celebration of the superhero movie – those crazy, often over-hyped films of selfless world-protectors and deadly avengers that brighten up the summer blockbuster season and Christmas television schedules. Though they may not always deliver on their promise, they are rarely less than entertaining and any genre that boasts films such as *Superman*, *The Incredibles*, *Batman Begins*, *X-Men*, *Spider-Man* and *Unbreakable* amongst its ranks is one worth celebrating.

So don your finest cape and fasten your utility belt as you prepare to enter the world of the superhero movie.

The Last Son of Krypton,
Earth's First Superhero

In the opening moments of Richard Donner's *Superman*, revered scientist and Superman's father Jor-El condemns three criminals to the Phantom Zone, a jail shaped like a pane of glass. Just as these Kryptonians are damned to their two-dimensional prison, another would escape his. Superman broke free of the comic-book page to arrive on the cinema screen 40 years after he was first created by writer/artist team Jerry Siegel and Joe Shuster; and in doing so, the last son of Krypton became cinema's first superhero. This was not the first time Superman had ventured outside his native medium, having appeared in a number of small-screen, radio and cinema-serial adaptations, most notably the excellent Max Fleischer-animated shorts of the 1940s and the George Reeves-starring serials of the 1950s. However, this was the first time the Man of Steel would be a star of the silver screen.

Yet Superman's transition to the big screen would not come in a single bound. Following the campy 1960s *Batman* television series, few were taking superheroes seriously and no studio was interested in making superhero movies. Nonetheless, following the success of *The Three Musketeers*, international producing team of father and son Alexander and Ilya Salkind, and Pierre Spengler acquired the rights from Warner Bros (who had owned DC comics since 1969) to produce a series of films based on Superman. The team went through a series of writers, with *The Godfather* scribe Mario Puzo delivering the final mammoth script, which the Salkinds decided to make as two films to be shot back-to-back. To bring credibility to the project, Marlon Brando was paid a then record $3.7 million for his extended cameo as Jor-El and Gene Hackman a none too miserly $2 million to play the villainous Lex Luthor. James Bond alumnus Guy Hamilton was hired to direct the films but, when the production moved to England, Hamilton, who was a UK tax exile, was forced to leave the project. A last-ditch attempt to find a replacement director proved to be the film's saving grace, with *Omen* director Richard Donner hired to shepherd the project. Locked into a tight schedule set by Brando and Hackman's shooting dates, Donner quickly hired long-time friend Tom Mankiewicz to give Puzo's script a heavy rewrite and instil a serious approach. As difficult as it was to find the crew behind the camera, the search for Superman himself proved even more exhaustive with every major Hollywood actor from Burt Reynolds to Nick Nolte reportedly turning down the part. In the end it was the 26-year-old unknown Christopher Reeve, in the dual roles of Clark Kent and Superman, who would make audiences believe a man could fly.

Filming under the banner of verisimilitude, Donner ensured *Superman* had an epic scope, from the Arthurian elegance of Krypton to the Norman Rockwell-inspired horizons of Smallville and the clamour of a 'great metropolitan newspaper'. This may have been a man who could fly but his feet were grounded in reality. Disagreement between Donner and the film's producers saw Donner unable to direct the sequel despite having already completed large portions of the film while working on *Superman*. The Salkinds then hired Richard Lester, a director with a more comedic approach, who had made their *Three Musketeers* pictures, to re-shoot much of Donner's work and complete the film. Fortunately, the theatrically released film contained enough of Donner's material to temper Lester's lighter touch, resulting in a worthy sequel. This was not the case for *Superman III*, a film directed solely by Lester, which opened on an extended slapstick routine and featured comedian Richard Pryor in a role almost as prominent as Christopher Reeve. The poor sequel undermined the esteem of the first film and was derided by fans and critics alike, but greater disappointment lay ahead. After an attempt by the Salkinds to create a Superman spin-off series starring Supergirl failed to take off at the box office, the Salkinds relinquished control of Superman only for purveyors of B-movie tat, Cannon Films, to pick up the rights. Cannon managed to lure Reeve back to the role by offering him greater creative control. Reeve wanted *Superman IV: The Quest for Peace* to be a more socially relevant adventure but how this translated into Superman flying a giant net full of the Earth's nuclear missiles into the sun is anyone's guess. The film, shot on a shoe-string budget – with many of the shoestrings clearly seen holding the Man of Steel up – was a major disappointment, sending Superman back to the Phantom Zone for the next 20 years. During these wilderness years many talented directors and Brett Ratner tried to get another Superman film made with wildly different approaches, but only by returning to Donner's original ideas and making a film that was a continuation of the two earlier films would Superman return under the watchful eye of Bryan Singer.

Though the new Superman film may have spent years condemned to development hell, it is not only the franchise that has often been considered 'cursed'. In the years following the suicide of television's first Superman, George Reeves, a fan superstition emerged known as the 'Superman curse'. The curse is said to befall anyone involved in adapting the Man of Steel, causing them to suffer from personal loss. The events surrounding Reeves' death would themselves form the basis of a film. *Hollywoodland*, starring superhero movie veteran Ben Affleck (*Daredevil*), an actor familiar with the pitfalls of typecasting, does not indulge in superstition. The film instead charts the decline of a pigeonholed actor, demonstrating how difficult it can be to step out of the Man of Steel's shadow. The most famous case of the supposed curse occurred when Christopher Reeve was paralysed from the neck down following a horse-riding accident in 1995. But, dispelling any myth, Reeve exceeded his onscreen heroism, becoming a role model and raising awareness and funds for people with disabilities. Against all medical expectations, Reeve also regained feeling over his body and movement in his index finger. The actor even found time to return to *Smallville* for a recurring role in the hit teen-Superman series before his death in 2004.

The Superman curse highlights how far-reaching the Man of Steel has become, not just in cinema but in popular culture. In much the same way, Superman, as the first comic-book superhero, set the red-and-blue standard for all others; *Superman* and *Superman II* designed the template and raised the bar for every other superhero movie since, from *Batman*'s serious superhero approach to *The Matrix*'s messianic allegory and *Spider-Man*'s deft mix of romance and heroism. Donner's opening film was a genre-starter that succeeded in being faithful to the hero's many incarnations on the comic-book page and the TV screen, while adding its own layer to the myth. That superheroes, their comics, television series and movies continue to grow in the fertile soil laid down by Jerry Siegel and Joe Shuster and enriched by Richard Donner is a testament to the timelessness of the Man of Steel, and the continuing influence of Earth's first superhero.

Superman (1978)

Cast: Christopher Reeve (Superman/Clark Kent), Margot Kidder (Lois Lane), Gene Hackman (Lex Luthor), Marlon Brando (Jor-El), Ned Beatty (Otis), Valerie Perrine (Eve Teschmacher), Jackie Cooper (Perry White), Glenn Ford (Jonathan Kent), Terence Stamp (General Zod)

Crew: Richard Donner (Director), Mario Puzo (Story and Screenplay), David Newman, Leslie Newman and Robert Benton (Screenplay), Tom Mankiewicz (Screenplay-uncredited), Geoffrey Unsworth (Director of Photography), Stuart Baird and Michael Ellis (Co-Editors), John Williams (Score)
Created by: Jerry Siegel and Joe Shuster

Plot: When the eminent Kryptonian scientist Jor-El realises natural forces will soon destroy his planet, he is left with one option: to place his infant son aboard a craft bound for Earth. Crashing in Smallville, Kansas, the child is found by an elderly couple, Jonathan and Martha Kent. Years later, the boy, now called Clark, is a teenager forced to hide his Kryptonian 'gifts' from the world. Following Jonathan's death, a Kryptonian crystal leads Clark to the Arctic where it forms a large crystalline structure. Inside this fortress, an image of Jor-El teaches Clark about his Kryptonian heritage and his superhuman powers. After years of solitude, Clark flies from his fortress draped in a red cape.

Now operating under a guise of mild-mannered timidity, Clark Kent begins working as a reporter at the *Daily Planet* in Metropolis alongside hardnosed journalist Lois Lane. Clark as Superman announces his existence to the people of Earth by saving Lois from a failing helicopter. Superman follows this rescue with a spate of other super-heroic activities, igniting the public's interest. He gives Lois his first interview, telling her he is on Earth to fight for Truth, Justice and the American Way.

Criminal genius Lex Luthor reads Lois's story, and deduces that Kryptonite, radioactive pieces of Superman's homeworld, should kill him. As part of his new scheme, Luthor weakens Superman with Kryptonite before sending a missile to the San Andreas Fault, which he hopes will plunge California into the sea, making his worthless desert land expensive beachfront property. But Superman escapes, and, though the missile explodes, he quickly plunges into the Earth, resealing the fault and stopping the adverse effects of the earthquake. However, Lois is buried beneath the earth following a tremor, forcing a grief-stricken Superman to begin furiously flying around the planet, turning it back on its axis and reversing time. With Lois safe, Superman drops Luthor off at prison before ascending into the heavens as Earth's mightiest protector.

Trivia: In the scene where the teenage Clark races a train travelling through Smallville, the parents of the young Lois Lane, seen sitting in one of the carriages, are played by Kirk Alyn and Noel Neill, the actors who portrayed Superman and Lois Lane in Superman's first live-action serial in 1948.

When cast as Superman, the slight Christopher Reeve refused to wear padded muscle under the suit, instead undergoing an intensive two-month training regime in which he gained 30 pounds under the supervision of David Prowse, the 6' 7" bodybuilder-turned-actor who played Darth Vader in the original *Star Wars* films.

One of the many stipulations of Marlon Brando's contract ensured that the legendary actor was not expected to memorise his dialogue. The lines for the extended monologue in which Jor-El sends his son to Earth were hidden throughout the set for Brando to read, including on the baby's diaper.

What the critics said: 'Superman is a pure delight, a wondrous combination of all the old-fashioned things we never really get tired of: adventure and romance, heroes and villains, earthshaking special effects and – you know what else? Wit.' Roger Ebert, *Chicago Sun-Times*

'Christopher Reeve, the young actor chosen to play the lead, is the best reason to see the picture: he's immediately likable, with an open-faced, deadpan style that's just right for a windup hero.' Pauline Kael, *The New Yorker*

Superhero Archetype: Many of today's superheroes owe their existence to the Man of Steel. When Siegel and Shuster created Superman they established the red-and-blue print for other superheroes to follow, launching the superhero archetype to which many have since added their own inflection. Among the various elements of the time-tested archetype first found in Superman is the 'secret identity'. This superhero mainstay, and how it is diametrically opposed to the heroic identity, first began when the Man of Steel used the timid façade of Clark Kent to safeguard his identity. Superman also gave the genre its first love story; today Spider-Man may enjoy a sneaky upside-down tryst, but that's kidstuff compared to the Kryptonian Casanova's airborne first dates. Another Superhero motif originated by the Man of Steel is the antithetical nemesis whose villainy contrasts with the hero's piety, with Luthor's human greed the opposite of Superman's alien sacrifice.

Yet one area where Superman's archetype finds itself on shaky ground is in its lack of a clear heroic responsibility. Later heroes would be born of recognisable motivations, with Batman on a personal vendetta to rid Gotham of crime and Spider-Man trying to atone for his uncle's death. Yet Superman, landing on Earth, arbitrarily in America, chooses to fight for Truth, Justice and the American Way, with his farm-bound upbringing seemingly prohibiting him from considering an alternative. Donner's *Superman* attempts to give the character a clearer sense of purpose by overlaying the superhero adventure with overt messianic allegory, in having Jor-El send his only son to help Earth's people with the commandment, 'Live as one of them. They can be a great people, Kal-El, they wish to be. They only lack the light to show the way.' The film's biblical symbolism goes some way towards explaining Superman's saintly mission, but, with an unwavering dedication to defending his adopted home, Superman's motivations are clearly not of this Earth.

Verdict: Today Superman is as much a cinematic icon as he is a comic-book character, so it is amazing to think that, up to four decades after his first appearance on the comic-book page, Superman had yet to make the leap to the silver screen. But in the late 1970s, the success of *Star Wars* left audiences searching the skies for more heroes and Superman would be the first to answer the call. Upon its release, and in an effort to signal to the world its big-screen legitimacy, *Superman* was subtitled *Superman: The Movie*, but as soon as the first notes of John Williams' triumphant score rang through theatres no further concessions were necessary: *Superman* was a Movie! In fact *Superman* would prove to be such an Earth-shattering achievement that no superhero story would ever need to justify its place on celluloid again.

In following the Man of Steel's journey over three distinct acts from doomed infant to Earth's mightiest protector, *Superman* plays almost like a biopic of the mythological icon. Opening in the delicate crystalline world of Krypton, the film brims with religious symbolism and is lent a Shakespearean-like gravitas by Marlon Brando's Jor-El. It then turns to the knee-deep wheat fields of small-town USA, a tribute to Americana with its bucolic setting and endless pastoral vistas; while the final act, and the setting for the majority of the film's action, 'bustling Metropolis' – clearly 'bustling New York' with a disguise less convincing than Clark Kent's glasses – proved to be the perfect backdrop for the Man of Steel's rise to high-flying hero. All these aspects succeed in presenting fantasy as fact, in a celebration of American culture through one of its greatest myths.

Throughout its running time, Donner's film seldom puts a foot wrong, having barely aged in the 30 years since its release. Christopher Reeve is eternally endearing as the eponymous hero and his awkward alias, while Margot Kidder, though not possessing classical movie-star looks, has more than enough fire to make you believe Superman would turn back time for her. Gene Hackman's Luthor may seem a little tame by the standards of Batman's demented rogues gallery, and the film loses some of its lyricism once the mythological grandeur of Krypton gives way to the action-orientated spectacle of Metropolis, but these are minor grievances. The film's only real Kryptonite is Lois's mid-flight poetry during her date with Superman, which includes such wince-worthy rhymes as, 'Here I am like a kid out of school, holding hands with a god, I'm a fool.'

Airbound sonnets not withstanding, Richard Donner's film is a singular triumph, heralding a new era of superheroes on screen. *Superman* is not only a great superhero movie but a great cinematic achievement, one which on every revisit proves that the original is still the best.

POW!POW!POW!POW!POW!

Superman II (1980)

Cast: Christopher Reeve (Superman/Clark Kent), Margot Kidder (Lois Lane), Gene Hackman (Lex Luthor), Terence Stamp (General Zod), Sarah Douglas (Ursa), Jack O'Halloran (Non), Jackie Cooper (Perry White)

Crew: Richard Lester (Director), Richard Donner (Director-uncredited), Mario Puzo (Story and Screenplay), David Newman and Leslie Newman (Screenplay), Tom Mankiewicz (Screenplay-uncredited), Robert Paynter and Geoffrey Unsworth (Directors of Photography), John Victor-Smith (Editor), Ken Throne (Score)

Created by: Jerry Siegel and Joe Shuster

Plot: When terrorists use a hydrogen bomb to take over the Eiffel Tower, Superman arrives just in time to push the activated device into outer space. There it explodes, its shockwaves shattering the Phantom Zone prison containing the three Kryptonian criminals: General Zod, Ursa and Non.

On Earth, Lois is beginning to suspect that Clark and Superman are the same person. Her suspicions are confirmed when Clark burns his hand but is miraculously unhurt. Superman takes Lois to the Fortress of Solitude, where he reveals his past. As their relationship deepens, Superman makes the decision to give up his powers in order to be with Lois. At the same time, the Kryptonians arrive on Earth and begin to experiment with their powers as they make their way to America's leader in the White House. A de-powered Clark begins the journey home with Lois, but on the way learns that the world's leaders have abdicated control to Zod. Clark realises he must return to the Fortress of Solitude and regain his powers.

In the meantime, a recently escaped Luthor makes a deal with the Kryptonians to deliver Superman. He leads them to the *Daily Planet*, suggesting they use Lois to draw him out. Just in time, Superman arrives and begins to fight the Kryptonians across

Metropolis. The super-powered battle causes massive damage to the city and Superman, fearing for the safety of Metropolis's residents, retreats. But Luthor directs Zod and his cronies to the Fortress of Solitude, where Superman gains the upper hand by convincing the Krytonians to use a molecular chamber on him, which in fact steals their powers. The now vulnerable criminals attack Superman, but in their struggle they fall into the depths of the Fortress. Later at the *Daily Planet*, Lois and Clark decide that Clark must remain Superman and that their relationship can never be. Clark then kisses Lois, erasing her recent memories. Repairing the damage caused by Zod, Superman promises the President as he restores the American flag to the top of the White House, 'I won't let you down again.'

Trivia: Terence Stamp, who plays General Zod in the film, would later provide the voice of Jor-El in the young Superman television series *Smallville*. Christopher Reeve and Annette O'Toole (*Superman III*'s Lana Lang) would also appear in the television series, Reeve as scientist Dr Swann and O'Toole as Martha Kent.

Originally the ending of *Superman*, in which the Man of Steel turns back time by flying around the world, was meant to close *Superman II*, with Superman's time reversal undoing the damage to Earth caused by the Kryptonians and cleansing Lois's memories. The idea was incorporated into the first film when its completion became a priority for the producers. The sequence, as it was intended to be seen, can be found in *Superman II: The Richard Donner Cut*.

It was originally planned that the explosion from the missile that Superman diverts to outer space at the end of *Superman* would free the Phantom Zone prisoners. This opening is one of the many scenes, including the Marlon Brando footage, reinstated in the superior *Superman II: The Richard Donner Cut* available on DVD.

What the critics said: 'With his perfect pacing, elegant narrative design, and depth of characterisation, Richard Lester has made as good a matinee movie as could be imagined.' Dave Kehr, *Chicago Reader*

'*Superman II* deserves its place in the classic comic-book canon for showing that the Man of Steel is just as human as the rest of us.' Chris Hewitt, *Empire*

Superhero Archetype: Of all the relationships that pivot about the superhero in service of the archetype, none is more detrimental to the hero's quest than that of the superhero and their love interest. *Superman II* explores the full potential and potential dangers of a superhero flying head over heels in love. In the first film Lois, by fulfilling the role of the damsel in distress, allows Superman to see her as someone in need of saving first, and a woman second. But in *Superman II*, as their relationship deepens and Lois begins to assert herself, Superman is no longer able to sublimate his desire, and in a plot tactic that would later be recycled for *Spider-Man 2*, he chooses to give up his powers and purpose in order to be with the woman he loves. Of course this one simple, selfish action is at the expense of world safety, as Zod and his minions are free to wreak havoc, forcing Superman to quash his feelings in order to stop these space invaders. In the end, Superman realises he will have to remain an ever-focused avenger, using an amnesia-inducing kiss to rob Lois of her memories and himself of love, returning to his Fortress of Solitude alone.

Verdict: While superhero movie sequels aim to provide twice the excitement of the originals, they usually don't require two directors to achieve this. However, *Superman II*'s now infamous production is a tale of two directors. Richard Donner was originally due to shoot both Superman movies in tandem, but budget and time constraints forced him to concentrate on *Superman*, with reportedly 75% of the sequel complete. When disagreements arose between Donner and *Superman*'s producers, the director was replaced by Richard Lester, director of the Beatles' films *A Hard Day's Night* and *Help!* Lester re-shot the majority of Donner's work with the notable exception of Gene Hackman's scenes, as the actor would not return for re-shoots. The resulting film should have been a fractured mess, but is a surprisingly cohesive whole and high watermark for future super-sequels.

The sequel does not have the galaxy-hopping scope of *Superman*'s origin story, but what it lacks in size it makes up for in power; Superman must protect Earth from an alien invasion from his home planet. The three Kryptonian villains, led by Terence Stamp's coolly reserved General Zod, face Superman head-on, and, unlike Hackman's evasive schemer Luthor, finally test the Man of Steel's mettle, culminating in an extended mêlée across Metropolis; a battle royale with enough clever choreography and visual quirkiness to still impress in today's computer-generated landscape, putting *Superman Returns*' giant glowing rock to shame. While Christopher Reeve again excels, flitting between his two roles, and Superman's deepening relationship with Lois is both credible and compelling, it is these scenes of Kryptonian carnage that give the film its super-power.

Some unexplained story elements such as Superman's amnesia-inducing kiss and the ultimate fates of the Krypton three detract from the finished film, but this sequel proved there were still many more cinematic skies for Superman to fly.

Pow!Pow!Pow!Pow!

Superman Returns (2006)

Cast: Brandon Routh (Superman/Clark Kent), Kate Bosworth (Lois Lane), Kevin Spacey (Lex Luthor), James Marsden (Richard White), Parker Posey (Kitty), Frank Langella (Perry White), Sam Huntington (Jimmy Olsen)

Crew: Bryan Singer (Director/Story), Michael Dougherty and Dan Harris (Story and Screenplay), Newton Thomas Sigel (Director of Photography), Elliot Graham and John Ottman (Co-

Editors), John Ottman (Score)

Created by: Jerry Siegel and Joe Shuster

Plot: A small craft crashes on a Kansas farm. Inside, the last son of Krypton, now the adult Superman, has returned to Earth. For the past five years Superman has been travelling through space in search of Krypton, only to find a 'graveyard'. In the guise of Clark Kent, Superman returns to his old job at the *Daily Planet*, where life has moved on without him – Lois Lane now has a son, Jason, and a fiancé, Richard. Meanwhile, the intrepid reporter herself is covering the launch of a new space shuttle. At the same time, Luthor, having returned from Superman's Fortress of Solitude, begins experimenting with stolen Kryptonian crystals, plunging the city into a blackout. As Lois's plane falls to Earth, Superman rushes to the rescue, eventually putting the craft down in a busy baseball stadium to the cheers of the crowd.

Though *Daily Planet* editor Perry White wants his reporters to cover Superman's return, Lois is more interested in the blackout. Her investigation brings her to Lex Luthor's home where she and her son are kidnapped by Luthor, who takes them out to sea on his yacht. The criminal genius explains his plan to build a new continent from a Kryptonite-infused crystal, which will plunge the United States under water and kill billions. Luthor shoots the crystal into the water where it quickly expands. Lois manages to fax her longitudinal coordinates to the *Daily Planet* but is subsequently set upon by one of Luthor's henchmen. However, the henchman is crushed by a piano, which Jason pushes with super-human strength. Lois and Jason are left on the sinking yacht as Luthor escapes to his new land mass. Upon seeing the fax, Richard goes to save Lois in his plane. With the adverse effects of Luthor's machinations on Metropolis quelled, Superman arrives to save Richard, Lois and Jason from the sinking yacht. The family safe, Superman confronts Luthor but Kryptonite in the ground robs him of his powers and he is beaten and thrown into the sea. Richard returns in his plane and Lois rescues Superman from the water. After recharging in the sun's rays, Superman dives into the Earth, loosening the newly formed land mass, which he then hurls into space.

Following his exertion and the exposure to Kryptonite, Superman falls lifeless to Metropolis where he remains in a coma. Lois visits him in the hospital and tells him her secret. Later, the revived Superman visits Jason's bedside and passes on his father's words, 'You will make my strength your own… the son becomes the father and father becomes the son,' before flying into the night sky.

Trivia: The many directors attached to a new Superman film prior to *Superman Returns* included Tim Burton with Nicolas Cage to play Superman, Brett Ratner and McG, while Kevin Smith and JJ Abrams wrote drafts of the script. Ironically, after vacating the *X-Men* director's chair, Singer was eventually replaced by Brett Ratner.

The last line of the final Reeve-starring Superman film, *Superman IV: The Quest for Peace*, is Superman saying to Luthor, after returning him to prison, 'See you in twenty.' It would be almost 20 years after the film was released in 1987 that Superman would return in 2006.

Brandon Routh and Kate Bosworth, who play the adult Superman and Lois Lane in *Superman Returns*, are in fact two and five years younger respectively than Tom Welling and Erica Durance, who play the young versions of these characters on the television series *Smallville*.

What the critics said: 'Singer's formula is finely balanced – nostalgia, high-end action/FX and classic characters. A warm rebirth for Krypton's favourite son.' Rob James, *Total Film*

'For all the pizzazz of *Superman Returns*, its global weapon of choice would not be terrorism, or nuclear piracy, or dirty bombs. It would be real estate.' Anthony Lane, *New Yorker*

Superhero Archetype: Among the many facets of the superhero archetype set by Superman is the tenet of the secret identity as a secondary personality in the shadow of the more dominant superhero persona; but lately this duality has come under threat. From the early Jerry Siegel and Joe Shuster comics, through the 1950s serials and up to the Christopher Reeve films, Superman has always been the dominant personality, with mild-mannered Clark Kent the masquerade. This ruse, though effective in hiding his secret identity, carries with it a Kryptonian criticism of humanity, with the Clark Kent persona Superman's view of mankind. This 'criticism' was most colourfully pointed out by pop-culturist and superhero aficionado Quentin Tarantino in his script for *Kill Bill*. In *Kill Bill* the eponymous assassin makes the point, 'Superman was born Superman. His alter-ego is Clark Kent. What Kent wears – the glasses, the business suit – that's the costume. That's the costume that Superman wears to blend in with us. Clark Kent is how Superman views us. He's weak, he's unsure of himself, he's a coward. Clark Kent is Superman's critique on the whole human race.'

This predominance of the Superman persona over Clark Kent continued until 1986 when the character's origin was amended and contemporised by writer John Byrne in the six-part comic *Man of Steel*. This process, known as retroactive continuity or ret-conning, saw Clark Kent elevated to the dominant personality, with Superman now the guise. This change in dynamics continued into future adaptations: *Lois and Clark*, *Superman: The Animated Series* and *Smallville*. However, the Christopher Reeve films, beginning before this retconning, always portrayed Superman as the real person, even if there were indications in *Superman II* of who Clark Kent could be in a world without Superman. In spite of the comics' rebalancing of these personas, *Superman Returns*, a film indebted to Donner's original, continues the more classic view of the superhero/secret identity dynamic with Brandon Routh playing Superman as the true identity, while bumbling Kent is the mask. In maintaining this dynamic, the hero sacrifices his chance for happiness with Lois, dismissing timid Clark as a friend, proving the adage 'nice guys finish last'.

Verdict: It is a testament to the universal popularity of the Man of Steel that when Bryan Singer came to make the first Superman film in almost two decades he felt confident that no back-story was necessary. Seemingly, if you know the name, then you know the story. One would expect that by eschewing the traditional origin story and presenting the Last Son of Krypton's as a *fait accompli*, the film would delve straight into the action, but *Superman Returns* takes a more languid approach, allowing audiences to get reacquainted with cinema's first superhero as superbly brought to life by Brandon Routh. In being a newcomer, Routh, like Christopher Reeve before him, is able to seamlessly embody the role without any superstar baggage. Taking his cues from Reeve's performance, he instils Superman with a hero's sincerity while making Kent awkwardly affable.

It is not only the new Kal-El who is indebted to Richard Donner's *Superman*, with the film opening on John Williams' majestic score and infused with the original's unabashed celebration of Americana. Though harking back to different eras, the film benefits from twenty-first-century technology, be it the computer-generated resurrection of Marlon Brando's Jor-El; close-ups of bullets bouncing not only off the Man of Steel's chest but now also his unblinking eye; and Superman looking like a bug on a windshield while heroically stopping a crashing plane.

While many of the Donner appropriations benefit Singer's film, the director would have been better advised to reference the comic book's ruthless businessman, rather than Gene Hackman's more tongue-in-cheek criminal genius, for Lex Luthor. Kevin Spacey does well investing the character with menace in his one meagre scene opposite the Big Blue Boy Scout, but is let down by a character whose plan to take over the world could have been hatched by Pinky and the Brain.

As in Donner's original, *Superman Returns* focuses on the relationship between Lois and Superman. But this never-can-be romance was so fully explored in the originals that there is very little left for these star-crossed lovers to do except indulge in some nostalgic flying across the city, while the decision to make Lois a mother has diminished much of her spark. This emphasis on human interactions would have been welcome had they been allied to superhuman heroics, but the film's climax fails to live up to the promise of the earlier action sequences, with Superman versus a giant glowing rock a misuse of the Man of Steel's first foray into the digital age.

Where *Superman Returns* succeeds most is in its lavish visuals, from Metropolis – no longer a thinly veiled New York – to the sumptuous views of Superman flying at night. Singer successfully manages to return Superman to the ranks of the superhero pantheon; a more 'super' sequel should see him fly back to his rightful place at the top.

Pow!Pow!Pow!Pow!

Supermen with Feet of Clay

Being a superhero seems like a sweet gig; cavorting in spandex, saving the girl and enjoying cups of hot cocoa around the Hall of Justice with Batman and Wonder Woman. However, as with any great job, your personal life is sure to suffer, and superhero movies excel at making these caped wonders pay for their high-flying fun. Thus, beneath their masks, superheroes are generally revealed to be a bunch of orphans, social outcasts and disfigured freaks, equally cursed and blessed by their powers. This group, plagued by misery, riddled with doubt and prone to dangerous pride and zealous greed, may be supermen, but they are supermen with feet of clay – well, except one.

Superman's powers may make him a god but it is his restraint in using them that makes him a saint. In *Superman,* the future Man of Steel, upon developing his powers, does not use his other-worldly gifts to make himself the high-school quarterback or the most popular kid in Smallville; instead he hides the power of a sun beneath his button-down collar, waiting patiently until adulthood when he can selflessly use his gifts in defence of Truth, Justice and the American Way. A model child and a testament to the benefits of a farm-bound Kansas upbringing, Superman is clearly from a different planet. What teenager, what adult for that matter, would not indulge in their newfound powers to improve their lot in life? It is these human indulgences that give us the Supermen with Feet of Clay, with Spider-Man one of the earliest trendsetters in this concrete footwear.

In *Spider-Man*, Peter Parker is a textbook nerd and the butt of his classmates' jokes. So when an errant, irradiated spider imbues him with an arsenal of new abilities, it is unsurprising that, instead of helping cats out of trees, Peter spends his first super-powered day knocking out the school bully, making moves on the girl of his dreams and planning ways to use his 'gifts' to make some extra cash. What is truly amazing about Spider-Man is that he completes all these hormonally charged feats with only the proportionate strength of a spider; imagine what he would have done if he had been given near-omnipotent Kryptonian powers for a day. Peter Parker, of course, is not a bad kid, but no amount of Uncle Ben's homespun wisdom is going to keep him from revelling in his gifts. However, with Peter's pride must come the fall. The guilt over his uncle's death, a death in which his indulgences are partly complicit, sets Peter on a diligent, heroic course in which he comes to the resolution: 'This is my gift, my curse. Who am I? I'm Spider-Man.'

The webbed wonder is not the only one to quickly learn that being a hero is a double-edged sword. Most superheroes would lay claim to being equally cursed and blessed by their powers, but the hero with the most justifiable grievance is surely the Incredible Hulk. Wolverine may have metal claws springing from his fists and the Fantastic Four's Thing may be permanently encrusted in a rocky acne, but these afflictions pale next to Bruce Banner's woes – popping out of his purple trunks like some steroidal sweetcorn mascot at the slightest irritation. As Kermit the Frog once sang, 'It's not easy being green.'

The Hulk is one member of the superhero fraternity who could easily be categorised as a monster had his comic-book roots not branded him a hero first. This was a role the not-so-jolly green giant had difficulty pursuing in his first big-screen adaptation. In *Hulk,* the green goliath does manage to save his ex-girlfriend from a pack of hybrid mutant dogs and settle some issues with his bent-on-destruction father, but it's hard to stop and save cats from trees when the villagers are chasing you with flaming torches and pitchforks. The Hulk, like all good movie monsters, is not evil, he is just misunderstood, and hopefully the upcoming Edward Norton-starring *The Incredible Hulk* should provide an opportunity to see the heroic Hulk, and prove that green is not always mean.

It is not only prideful indulgences and monster mash-ups that weigh these heroes down; some simply prefer to keep their feet on the ground. *Unbreakable*, M Night Shyamalan's original super-hero tale, features a hero – in what could be considered a more realistic reaction to gaining superpowers – choosing to repress his abilities and live an ordinary, if unfulfilling, life. David Dunn is crippled with self-doubt, but when events conspire to force him to accept his heroic calling he takes on the mantle of the hero, proving, like Spider-Man and the Hulk before him, that, despite any fear, pride or monstrous misunderstandings, given the oppor-tunity, these Supermen with Feet of Clay can still fly.

Unbreakable (2000)

Cast: Bruce Willis (David Dunn), Samuel L Jackson (Elijah Price), Robin Wright Penn (Audrey Dunn), Spencer Treat Clark (Joseph Dunn), Charlayne Woodard (Elijah's Mother), Johnny Hiram Jamison (Young Elijah), Chance Kelly (Orange Suit Villain)

Crew: M Night Shyamalan (Director/Writer), Eduardo Serra (Director of Photography), Dylan Tichenor (Editor), James Newton Howard (Score)

Created by: M Night Shyamalan

Plot: On the surface there is nothing special about security guard David Dunn. He is going through a messy separation from his wife Audrey, with his son Joseph stuck in the middle – an ordi-nary man, leading an ordinary life. That is until he becomes the sole survivor of a horrific train crash. The 'accident', though claiming the lives of 131 people, leaves David miraculously unharmed. After the crash, David begins to question himself and his life.

Shortly after, David is approached by Elijah, the owner of an art gallery that trades in comic art originals. Elijah suffers from a rare genetic defect that causes his bones to shatter easily and appears to provide David with the answers he is looking for. He tells him that they are at opposite ends of the same spectrum; that in every way he is physically fallible, David is unbreakable. Elijah explains he has come to this conclusion by studying comic books. David is initially hesitant to believe Elijah's claims but he soon begins to test his limitations, bench-pressing more weights than ever before and experimenting with his seemingly extra-sensory ability to sense danger. David finally begins to believe Elijah's claims; wrapping himself in his security poncho (essentially his cape and cowl), he goes out to right wrongs, which culminates in a fight with an orange-suited man who has taken a family hostage. David succeeds in killing the kidnapper and in doing so takes on the mantle of a hero. As a result of discovering his true calling, David finds contentment in his home life, reconciling with his wife.

Finally at peace, David visits Elijah, who he now considers a friend, to thank him for all he has done; but upon shaking his hand David learns Elijah's terrible secret. Elijah caused David's train crash and a number of other fatal 'accidents' in order to unearth a hero, thus giving his life purpose. As Elijah remarks, 'Now that we know who you are, I finally know who I am. I am not a mistake.' The story ends with David leaving Elijah, who is later (in typical supervillain fashion) incarcerated in an insane asylum.

Trivia: On the *Unbreakable* DVD Special Features, Samuel L Jackson explains that he chose the purple colour scheme for Elijah as he felt it befitted the regal nature of the character. The actor also chose purple as the colour of his lightsaber for his role of Jedi Knight Mace Windu in the *Star Wars* prequels.

M Night Shyamalan has a habit of turning up on screen in his own films. In *The Sixth Sense* he played a doctor, and in *Lady in the Water* he took the self-aggrandising role of an author whose writings would change the world. For *Unbreakable,* Shyamalan plays a suspected drug-dealer questioned by Bruce Willis's David Dunn.

When Marvel Comics contemporised many of its long-standing characters in what became known as the 'Ultimate Universe', eyepatch-sporting super-spy Nick Fury was modelled, with the actor's consent, on *Unbreakable* star Samuel L Jackson. Though the more traditional version of the character was brought to television screens in an unsuccessful pilot starring David Hasselhoff, it will be Jackson and not the Hoff who will play Fury in the upcoming *Iron Man* movie.

What the critics said: 'The presence of pop-culture references via comics makes quite notable the absence of any humour or sense of fun, just as it makes its pretentions to deep meaning and self-importance all the more specious.' Todd McCarthy, *Variety*

'Many viewers won't be able to get past the premise... but Shyamalan tackles his idea with almost no irony. Willis plays the realisation that he might be set apart from humanity with a quivering uncertainty, strikingly at odds with the bright-coloured glee of a Marvel or DC character.' Kim Newman, *Empire*

Superhero Archetype: *Unbreakable* diligently follows the superhero archetype, as it does the many tropes of the genre. David Dunn's origin is parallel to that of the antithetical villain Elijah (they are on 'opposite ends of a spectrum'), while at the same time Elijah's actions (the train crash) cause the origin of the hero's responsibility. Furthermore, there exists a distinct duality between David Dunn's secret and hero identities; the film goes to pains to illustrate how Dunn is an ordinary man, thus accentuating the extraordinary aspect of his heroic power. Even Dunn's allies follow the genre prerequisites laid down in the archetype: his wife (love interest) never discovers Dunn's powers throughout the film; however, Dunn does confide in his son (sidekick) by the film's close. By placing the superhero archetype in a realistic context, the film manages to tap into a rich vein of superhero mythos often overlooked by the more blockbuster-orientated superhero fare.

Verdict: *Unbreakable* is an oddity amongst superhero movies. Though not based on any comic book, it adheres more rigidly to the tenets of the superhero genre and the larger comic medium than most adaptations. From the smallest details (alliteration of the hero's name) to the larger character types (an antithetical villain), the film displays an understanding and reverence for superhero lore. Littered with self-referential dialogue, the film never allows its prescribed source to overwhelm the reality of the piece, rather allowing the audience, along with the film's protagonist, to slowly realise they are in a superhero movie. Thus, when Elijah is revealed in the film's climax to be the villain, the audience, much like the hero, is astonished for not recognising it earlier.

Unbreakable's comic-book fidelity is not confined to the plot, with Shyamalan clearly emulating a comic-book aesthetic. Many scenes take place with little or no cuts and the action is sparingly fitted onto the screen, thereby mirroring a comic panel's economic use of space. Furthermore, the characters all appear according to their generic types, with Samuel L Jackson playing Elijah as a lonely and bitter soul – the character's 'disproportionate' head on a spindly frame a million miles away from *Pulp Fiction*'s Jules – and the hero David Dunn played with honesty and self-doubt by that most square-jawed of actors, Bruce Willis.

That Shyamalan manages to fully create, in story and image, a superhero world without ever faltering in the film's verisimilitude is a credit to his skill as a filmmaker. A deftly made, engaging work that celebrates the best of superheroes, this film resonates long after its initial viewing. *Unbreakable* joins *The Incredibles* in being among the best superhero movies not based on a comic book.

POW!POW!POW!POW!

Spider-Man (2002)

Cast: Tobey Maguire (Spider-Man/Peter Parker), Kirsten Dunst (Mary Jane Watson), Willem Dafoe (Green Goblin/Norman Osborn), James Franco (Harry Osborn), Cliff Robertson (Ben Parker), Rosemary Harris (May Parker), JK Simmons (J Jonah Jameson)

Crew: Sam Raimi (Director), David Koepp (Writer), Don Burgess (Director of Photography), Arthur Coburn and Bob Murawski (Co-Editors), Danny Elfman (Score)

Created by: Stan Lee and Steve Ditko

Plot: When Peter Parker, a lonely teen living in a New York suburb is bitten by a genetically modified spider, he soon develops the arachnid's proportionate abilities. With these new-found talents, Peter enters a wrestling competition for the cash he needs to buy a car, which he hopes will impress the girl of his dreams, Mary Jane. Wearing a makeshift red-and-blue outfit, Peter is christened 'Spider-Man' by the tournament announcer. Spider-Man easily wins the wrestling match but the organiser refuses to pay him the full money. As the disgruntled teen leaves, the organiser is robbed, but Peter, with the opportunity to stop the thief, gets his revenge by letting him go. Later Peter's uncle is shot and killed by the same thief, causing Peter to reconsider how he should use his powers.

Soon after, Peter graduates from high school and moves to the city with his friend Harry, whose father Norman Osborn is a businessman and scientist charged with developing technology for the military. Recently Osborn has begun using an artillery-laden glider and suit to become the Green Goblin, killing anyone who threatens his business interests. Meanwhile Peter, who is now working as a freelance photographer for the *Daily Bugle* newspaper, continues to atone for his uncle's death by fighting crime in his Spider-Man guise. Spider-Man and the Goblin soon cross paths when the now-mad scientist attacks a city fair. This prompts a series of fights between the Goblin and Spider-Man.

Meanwhile, Peter/Spider-Man and Mary Jane's relationship deepens when Spider-Man saves her from a street gang. This rescue culminates in Mary Jane kissing Spider-Man while he hangs upside down from a web. However, the Goblin discovers Spider-Man's identity and kidnaps Mary Jane, holding her and a railcar full of children hostage atop the Queensboro Bridge. Spider-Man manages to save them all and fights the Goblin one last time. The conflict ends with the Goblin, hoping to impale Spider-Man on his glider, inadvertently stabbing and killing himself. Peter returns Osborn's body to his home where Harry is waiting. But, on seeing Spider-Man, Harry assumes he is the killer and vows at his father's graveside to make Spider-Man pay. Mary Jane reveals her true feelings to Peter, but he hides his, knowing how dangerous his identity as Spider-Man can be to the people he loves. As he walks away, he finally understands his uncle's words, 'With great power comes great responsibility.'

Trivia: When testing his organic web-shooters, Peter tries a number of superhero catchphrases to get them to work, including 'Up, up and away' from *Superman* and 'Shazam', the incantation of Captain Marvel.

An early teaser trailer for *Spider-Man* featured a helicopter flown by armed robbers being trapped in a web spun between the twin towers of the World Trade Centre. The scenes and any major shots of the World Trade Centre were removed from the final film following the terrorist attacks of September 11, but the towers can be seen reflected in Spider-Man's eyes during the montage where Spider-Man first comes to New York City.

The iconic rain-drenched kiss between an upside-down Spider-Man and Mary Jane has been parodied in television series and films such as *The OC, Shrek 2* and, of course, *The Simpsons*.

What the critics said: 'The best part of *Spider-Man* comes between the spider bite and Peter's discovery of his calling, when the movie asks us to imagine what a retiring, middle-class teenager would do with superhuman powers.' AO Scott, *New York Times*

'Charming with a perpetual look of startled bewilderment at the super powers he possesses, Maguire is perfect as an ordinary guy with a big secret.' Kirk Honeycutt, *The Hollywood Reporter*

Superhero Archetype: In the early days of caped crusaders, an intrinsic part of the superhero archetype was the sidekick – adolescents who diligently followed their heroes around with matching costumes and comic asides. These mini-supermen, such as Robin (Batman), Bucky (Captain America) and Snapper Carr (Justice League of America), provided young comic readers with a character with whom they could identify and the writers an easy means of exposition – as the hero stopped at every major narrative juncture to explain, for the benefit of his short-pants assistant and the reader at home, what was going on.

However, in the 1960s these Identification-Boys and Exposition-Lads found themselves out of work. This unemployment did not come from a tightening of child labour laws but rather through the integration of the superhero and his sidekick into a singular persona. Stan Lee closed a spider's web around these two characters and from this cocoon the Friendly Neighbourhood Spider-Man emerged. Spider-Man was a teen hero who young readers could relate to, and with a propensity for talking to himself he was able to handle his own exposition.

Spider-Man continues with this full-service hero, as Tobey Maguire's webbed wonder is a hero beset by recognisable problems, whose moments of introspective voiceover provide all the exposition an audience would need. In essence, Spider-Man is a hero who is his own sidekick. Well, it is easier to multi-task when you have eight limbs.

Verdict: Spider-Man is a child of the 1960s. That is not to say he was the product of some marijuana-infused, hippie love-in, but rather the creation of two comic-book creators, writer Stan Lee and artist Steve Ditko, who were still enjoying the upswing of the swinging sixties. It was a time when high-school bullies could still be tough despite ridiculous monikers like Flash Thompson, and caring aunts would have apple-pie waiting when you got home from school. So it surprised many, after the doom and gloom of *Batman*, *Blade* and *X-Men*, that Sam Raimi, a director who had already displayed his superhero dark side with *Darkman*, chose to draw his inspiration from these early years rather than later comic stories mired by clones, dead girlfriends and alien symbiotes. In doing so he produced a film that was sweet but never saccharine, comic without being camp, and playful but never at the expense of story or character. And, for Spider-Man, character is key.

As a long-time Spider-Man fan, Raimi understood that the success of the comics lay not in the superhero, but in the secret identity, with Peter Parker's struggle with his 'Power and Responsibility' the most important ingredient of his 40-year mythos. Thus, the casting of the bespectacled Peter and not the costume-covered hero was a priority for Raimi, with the director making the then unlikely choice of art-house favourite Tobey Maguire. Having already proved his apple-pie credentials in *Pleasantville*, Maguire was more than equal to the task of embodying the good-natured Peter, with a deft mix of computer pixels, stuntmen and his toned-up physique filling out the hero's long-johns.

Supporting Maguire as the perpetually-in-distress Mary Jane, Kirsten Dunst turned in an earnest performance despite some cheddary dialogue, while her swinging-in-the-rain, upside-down kiss with Spider-Man remains one of the most iconic superhero movie moments. However, it is Willem Dafoe's Green Goblin who steals the show. Cackling like the Wicked Witch of the West while looking like a Power Ranger, Dafoe's icy stare and commitment to the role ensured that the Goblin was a worthy first foe for the costumed web-slinger. In truth, the villain is so effective that, by the film's close, the audience is left wanting more entan-

glements with the webbed wonder; however, the long but necessary origin story means that *Spider-Man* remains a tasty entrée
ahead of the greater fulfilment of Spidey's second swing.

POW!POW!POW!POW!

Hulk (2003)

Cast: Eric Bana (Hulk/Bruce Banner), Jennifer Connelly (Betty
Ross), Sam Elliott (General Thaddeus 'Thunderbolt' Ross), Josh
Lucas (Major Glenn Talbot), Nick Nolte (Absorbing Man/David
Banner), Paul Kersey (Young David Banner), Cara Buono (Edith
Banner)

Crew: Ang Lee (Director), James Schamus (Story and Screenplay),
Michael France and John Turman (Screenplay), Frederick Elmes
(Director of Photography), Tim Squyres (Editor) Danny Elfman
(Score)

Created by: Stan Lee and Jack Kirby

Plot: Bruce Krenzler (né Banner) is an emotionally remote
geneticist, exploring cellular regeneration with his research
partner and ex-girlfriend Betty Ross. When a lab accident
exposes Bruce to lethal amounts of gamma radiation, he wakes in
a hospital feeling better than he ever has before. He is visited by
his biological father David Banner, who tells him that when
Bruce was a child he altered his DNA. Later, as Bruce sleeps,
various stresses and anxieties converge on his subconscious,
prompting him to physically transform into a seemingly mindless,
green behemoth. This Hulk destroys much of the hospital and
Bruce's lab. When he wakes the next morning, Bruce has no
memory of the night before. He is visited by Betty's father, Army
General Thunderbolt Ross, who suspects that Bruce was involved
in the destruction of his lab and places him under house arrest.
  Meanwhile, David, deeming Betty to be a threat to the culmi-
nation of his experiments, sends a pack of mutant dogs to kill her,

but the Hulk comes to her rescue. Later, Ross arrives and captures Bruce, who has returned to his human form, taking him to an underground laboratory where military scientist Major Talbot tries to extract samples from the Hulk. But the unleashed Hulk escapes the lab and begins a cross-country trek, pursued by the military, home to Betty. The constant attacks from the army only serve to anger the Hulk, sustaining him. Realising this, Betty goes to San Francisco where the Hulk's rampage has taken him; there, she calms the Hulk, enabling him to revert back to Bruce.

In the meantime, David has been experimenting further, imbuing himself with the power to absorb the properties of any material he touches. He turns himself over to the military on the condition that he sees Bruce one more time. At this meeting, David tries to goad Bruce into releasing the Hulk so that he may absorb his power. Eventually, David bites into an electricity cable, taking on its properties. As the father becomes a large electrical being, the son transforms into the Hulk. The two fight, with David trying to absorb the Hulk's energy, but the power is too much for him to bear. At the same time, Ross orders a gamma strike; the explosion kills David while Bruce is left lifeless in a nearby lake. One year later, Ross believes Bruce is dead; however, deep in the jungle Bruce is administering medicine to the poor. When militia arrive, Bruce warns them, 'You're making me angry.' Soon after, a primal roar is heard across the jungle.

Trivia: Superhero creator Stan Lee makes another trademark cameo in *Hulk*. This time he plays a security guard alongside Lou Ferrigno, the actor who played Hulk in *The Incredible Hulk* television series (1978-1982) and subsequent TV movies.

Director Ang Lee himself performed much of the motion-captured actions that Industrial Light and Magic (ILM) technicians used as reference points to animate the computer-generated Hulk.

In *Hulk,* Bruce Banner's father is named David in reference to *The Incredible Hulk* television series in which Bruce Banner's name was changed to David Bruce Banner. The role was played by Bill Bixby who died of cancer in 1993.

What the critics said: 'For all their considerable entertainment value, the two *X-Men* outings and *Spider-Man* (2002) are essentially high-school capers. *Hulk* is no less enjoyable, but it's in another league of complexity and for this reason is the best Marvel adaptation so far.' Rob White, *Sight and Sound*

'Incredibly long, incredibly tedious, incredibly turgid.' AO Scott, *New York Times*

Superhero Archetype: The Hulk is not your typical superhero, forgoing the mask, cape and spandex (although his purple pants are super-elastic); he is a no-frills monster striving to survive. Yet throughout his comic and television incarnations, he has been cast in the role of a hero, a mantle he picks up once more for his first big-screen outing.

In *Hulk,* the green goliath fulfils the tenets of the superhero archetype as readily as any of his costume-clad colleagues, from the simple alliteration of the hero's name to his duality with the villain. Also, like many superheroes, the two events of the Hulk's origin, his power and heroic responsibility, are the direct result of the actions of his arch-nemesis, his father. The elder Banner not only gave his son powers through genetic-tinkering, but provided Bruce with an oedipal heroic responsibility when he murdered the future Hulk's mother. This act of violence instilled the psychological traumas that would later be the catalyst for Bruce's heroic transformation.

David also takes on the role of the mirror villain; both Banners, senior and junior, are geneticists, and whether by choice or by the sins of the father, they gained their ability to transform through scientific experimentation. David's descent into madness and villainy stands as an ever-present reminder to Bruce of the fate that awaits him should he ever submit to the monster within. Yet it seems, no matter how monstrous the appearance or misunderstood the man, the Hulk remains a hero.

Verdict: Despite sharing the surname Lee, there is little else that Hulk creator Stan and film director Ang have in common. Stan is a spinner of exciting comic-book tales of alliteratively named heroes imbued with fantastical powers, while Ang is the Oscar-winning director of period pieces (*Sense and Sensibility*) and controversy-baiting features (*Brokeback Mountain*). So when Ang Lee was chosen to wield the megaphone for the Hulk's first foray into feature films, the Taiwanese filmmaker was an unexpected, yet promising, choice. However, when the director of *The Ice Storm* was confronted with an unfamiliar monster, rather than fully embrace the beast, Lee chose to create a family drama with all the trappings of a superhero movie. This was a novel approach, but one whose execution proved more mutated than the eponymous monster.

Taking the 'Incredible' out of the *Hulk*, the film is primarily a Greek tragedy, with the first victim being any sense of wonder or superhero spectacle. To compensate for this temperate approach, the film foregrounds a disjointed 'comic-book' style of editing, but the effect is jarring and small recompense for the excitement that should be on the screen, not around it. One of the many ways in which *Hulk* tames this comic-book beast is in the hero's origin. In the comics, Bruce Banner becomes the Hulk when he is irradiated in the eye of a nuclear explosion, but in this adaptation it is a mundane laboratory accident that unleashes the beast.

The few thrills the film does offer are mixed. One scene, reminiscent of later monster movie *King Kong*, has the Hulk take on three assailants. But where Peter Jackson's Kong fended off T-Rexes in an expertly executed action scene, the green goliath only has to keep three badly rendered mutant mutts at bay. An extended cross-country mêlée, in which the army pursues the Hulk, does reach heroic heights, but remains unmatched in the rest of the film.

Surprisingly, in a film that favours human interaction over superhuman heroics, the script is as weak as the Hulk is strong, devoid of any warmth and humour. Detached characterisation does the cast few favours, with Bana struggling to fill the vacant

Banner with some personality and Betty Ross, coldly played by Jennifer Connelly, remaining unsympathetic throughout. Only Nick Nolte, as Banner's father and the Hulk's creator, seems comfortable flitting between family drama and superheroics. But these respected thespians are acted off the screen by the CGI Hulk, who has more pixel-infused personality than the principal actors combined.

The film is not without merit, but in striving for emotional realism, Lee populates his world with characters who, upon encountering the Hulk, are neither frightened nor amazed, instead viewing him as an everyday nuisance; an apathy that quickly spreads to the film's audience. In the end, *Hulk* is a superhero movie that should have been a rampaging monster but is instead full of puny humans.

Pow!Pow!Pow!

Spiderman 2 (2004)

Cast: Tobey Maguire (Spider-Man/Peter Parker), Kirsten Dunst (Mary Jane 'MJ' Watson), James Franco (Harry Osborn), Alfred Molina (Doctor Octopus/Otto Octavius), Rosemary Harris (May Parker), JK Simmons (J Jonah Jameson)

Crew: Sam Raimi (Director), Alfred Cough, Miles Millar and Michael Chabon (Story), Alvin Sargent (Screenplay), Bill Pope (Director of Photography), Bob Murawski (Editor), Danny Elfman (Score)

Created by: Stan Lee and Steve Ditko

Plot: In the years since Peter Parker first became Spider-Man, the webbed wonder has become a champion to the city; yet Peter still struggles with the burden of his 'Power and Responsibility'. His inability to be there for Mary Jane has frayed their relationship, while his college grades have started to suffer. In an effort to boost these falling test scores, Harry, who took over Osborn

Industries following his father's death, arranges for Peter to meet an eminent scientist in his employ, Dr Otto Octavius. Octavius has created a new machine that will produce renewable energy from the rare isotope, tritium. But at the first public testing the machine begins to dangerously malfunction, prompting Peter to don his Spider-Man guise to stop the test, but not before Octavius's wife is killed and the robotic arms that the doctor uses to operate the device are fused to his spine.

Octavius wakes in a hospital under the control of the robotic arms. Now consumed by the singular goal of completing his experiment, he escapes the hospital and soon his efforts to steal the necessary funds to rebuild his machine bring him into conflict with Spider-Man. Meanwhile, Peter has become crippled by his heroic responsibility and experiences trouble accessing his powers. When Peter discovers that MJ is set to marry another man, John Jameson, he vows to be 'Spider-Man no more'. Now free of his dual identity, Peter's grades begin to improve and he rekindles his relationship with MJ. However, needing tritium to power his machine, Octavius visits Harry, who promises to give it to him if Octavius can deliver Spider-Man alive so that Harry may exact his revenge for his father's death. Knowing that Peter takes photographs of Spider-Man, Octavius kidnaps MJ, warning Peter he will not let her go until Spider-Man faces him. Peter, as Spider-Man once more, confronts Octavius and a frantic fight on top of a speeding train ensues, with Octavius emerging the victor. He delivers Spider-Man to Harry in exchange for the tritium. But Harry is stunned to discover that Peter is Spider-Man. Peter wakes just in time to explain to Harry that, whatever issues exist between them, Octavius's machine could destroy the city.

Spider-Man goes to Octavius's dockside lair, where the mad scientist is keeping MJ and his machine, and engages him in battle for the final time. In the process, Spider-Man loses his mask but manages to end the robotic arms' control over Octavius, who, realising the error of his ways, drowns his dangerous machine and himself in the water. MJ, seeing that Peter is Spider-Man, understands his recent evasiveness but is still set to marry John.

However, on the day of her wedding, she runs from the church to Peter's apartment, where she professes her true feelings for him; but before Peter can respond, police sirens ring in the distance as MJ tells him, 'Go get 'em tiger.'

Trivia: Alfred Cough and Miles Millar, the creators of the Superman television series *Smallville*, and Michael Chabon, author of the Pulitzer Prize-winning novel *The Amazing Adventures of Kavalier & Clay*, are among the writers who contributed to the screenplay for *Spider-Man 2*.

Although briefly mentioned in the first film, *Spider-Man 2* marks the first appearance of Dr Curt Connors (Dylan Baker), a character who, in the comics, upon experimenting with regenerative lizard DNA to re-grow his lost arm, becomes the villain the Lizard – a role he may yet fill in future Spider-Man sequels.

Spider-Man 2 was originally to be called *The Amazing Spider-Man* in reference to the full title of the character's longest-running comic-book series.

What the critics said: '*Spider-Man 2* is the best superhero movie since the modern genre was launched with *Superman*.' Roger Ebert, *Chicago Sun-Times*

'Tobey Maguire now seems entirely comfortable filling Parker's shoes as well as the webbed suit, his hangdog expression demanding viewers' empathy.' James White, *Total Film*

Superhero Archetype: For all of Batman's claims of fighting a 'one-man war against crime', with a reliable butler, police commissioners willing to look the other way, and an assortment of Technicolor teen sidekicks, he has had a lot of help. To find a truly self-made (super)man, you have to look to Spider-Man. Peter Parker's progression from high-school loser to DIY superhero has been a hard-fought journey. Unlike Superman, who was handed the whole 'How to...' guide printed on green crystals – a veritable Kryptonian Wikipedia or Kryptopedia – the introvert teen, upon being unceremoniously bitten by a spider, had to experiment to discover his gifts. Even when he mastered these strange new abilities, he had no childhood alien cloth from which to spin his new costume, or subterranean rodent infestation to help inspire its design. Peter designed, stitched and sewed the suit himself, and, though not an expert seamster, he did a pretty good job, even if, by his own admission, it is 'kind of itchy and it rides up in the crotch a little bit, too'.

Finally, costume-clad and in control of his gifts, this woe-ridden wonder must have thought things were looking up, safe in the knowledge he would always have his trusty Uncle Ben to guide him. But fate threw him another setback as Ben was taken from him, leaving Peter with a survivor's complex and a dogmatic epitaph to live by. His Aunt May has not been much help either, her sermons and nostalgia little use against opponents such as Doctor Octopus and Goblin & Son. As for further allies, Spider-Man does not need a sidekick to crack wise, being well able to sling his own one-liners; and his team-up with an alien symbiote (in *Spider-Man 3*) does not end well. One would think his true love Mary Jane would be the light in his life, but she divides her time between ignoring Peter, moaning about her floundering career, cheating on him with Harry (in *Spider-Man 3*) and getting captured. Daredevil's girlfriend Elektra may have been a murderous ninja who died, but at least she never cavorted with the enemy behind his back.

Of all the supposedly 'lone' heroes protecting the Superverse, Spider-Man, pulling himself up by his webstrings and against all odds, is the one hero who can claim he did it all by himself; a true working-class (super)hero.

Verdict: Superheroes are a sequel-baiting bunch, promising never-ending crusades against crime; they run, fly and swing out of every film in search of their next adventure. The prevailing filmmaking theory for these further exploits seems to be: if it is film number two, all the elements from the original should be at least doubled.

If *Batman* had one villain, *Batman Returns* should have two; saving the city was fine for the *Fantastic Four,* but the sequel should see the quartet saving the world. Yet such multiplication can often yield muddled results and a weaker film. *Spider-Man 2* avoids this sequel blight (that would claim part three) by not wasting time trying to make everything bigger, but by making them better: better special effects, improved dialogue and more elaborate action sequences – even Mary Jane's hair has a more realistic hue.

The story may find our hero at the end of his web, struggling to juggle his dual identities, but the film's leading man is having no such worries. Tobey Maguire manages to give Peter a down-beaten, slapstick-lite charm, while his hero excels in derring-do, particularly in the trilogy's standout sequence – the train-top tussle with Doc Ock. Where this sequel really triumphs over its predecessor is that the laborious origin story is already spun, so the film can swing straight in, allowing events to unfold at an unfettered pace, with excellent action sequences interspersed by Peter and MJ's realistically rendered romance.

This tempo only slackens late in the second act, when Spider-Man suffers a superhero crisis of confidence, and languishes in a powerless daze, which even a pep talk from Aunt May, burning buildings and a number of ill-advised leaps from rooftops cannot shake. Thankfully, MJ's kidnapping is just what the doctor ordered, waking Spider-Man from his stupor in time for a thrilling third act. The MD in question is, of course, Doctor Octopus, who, like his predecessor the Green Goblin, manages to pilfer every scene he is in. However, unlike Willem Dafoe, Alfred Molina's villain is unencumbered by an all-covering suit, instead being free to infuse the character with so much villainous bravado that even his tentacles swing with an arrogant gait.

Following up a successful superhero movie is always a tightrope act across a pit of fan expectations, potentially stale characters and risky new elements. But Sam Raimi completes this vertigo-inducing feat with poise and grace, as *Spider-Man 2* is a close-to-perfect superhero movie, and first among sequels in the superhero movie canon.

Pow!Pow!Pow!Pow!Pow!

Spider-Man 3 (2007)

Cast: Tobey Maguire (Spider-Man/Peter Parker), Kirsten Dunst (Mary Jane 'MJ' Watson), James Franco (New Goblin/Harry Osborn), Thomas Haden Church (Sandman/Flint Marko), Topher Grace (Venom/Edward 'Eddie' Brock), Bryce Dallas Howard (Gwen Stacy), Rosemary Harris (May Parker), JK Simmons (J Jonah Jameson)

Crew: Sam Raimi (Director/Co-Writer), Ivan Raimi and Alvin Sargent (Co-Writers), Bill Pope (Director of Photography), Bob Murawski (Editor), Christopher Young (Score)

Created by: Stan Lee and Steve Ditko

Plot: Life is going well for Peter Parker and he feels the time is right to propose to Mary Jane. However, Peter's old friend Harry still blames him for his father's death and attacks Peter with his father's Goblin weapons, with Peter only narrowly managing to defeat this New Goblin. Later, at an upscale restaurant, Peter's planned proposal is interrupted when MJ tells him that she has been dropped from the musical in which she has been starring due to poor reviews. This prompts the couple to argue, with MJ leaving Peter alone at the table.

Peter is later contacted by the police who tell him that the man who killed his uncle was in fact Flint Marko. Marko, who has recently been imbued with sand-like properties after falling into a particle accelerator, is on the run from the law. Back at his apartment Peter is overcome by anger, motivating an alien symbiote to envelop him, turning his suit black and giving him enhanced powers that he uses to fight Marko, eventually drowning him in an underground tunnel. Spider-Man's woes do not end there, as rival photographer Eddie Brock falsifies pictures to make Spider-Man look like a criminal. Peter exposes the fraud and Brock is fired. Next, Harry attacks MJ, forcing her to end her relationship with Peter. Soon after, he tells Peter he has been having an affair with MJ. With his relationship over, Peter submits himself to the destructive power of the suit, attacking Harry and leaving him for dead. He then visits MJ at the club where she has been working, but a fight breaks out between Peter and club security in which MJ is accidentally hurt. Wracked with guilt, Peter goes to a church tower where the ringing bells allow him to remove the symbiote suit, which then binds with Eddie Brock below. The symbiote and Brock's joint hatred of Peter Parker sees them become Venom.

Venom kidnaps MJ and joins forces with Flint Marko. Knowing he cannot defeat them both, Peter appeals to Harry for help. He refuses, but Peter still goes to save MJ. With Spider-Man losing his fight against the villains, Harry on his Goblin glider arrives to help. Although they defeat Venom and save MJ, Harry is fatally wounded. Following his friend's demise, Peter returns to MJ's workplace, where she takes his hand once more.

Trivia: Spider-Man's comic-book co-creator Stan Lee completes his trilogy of cameos in *Spider-Man 3,* stopping to tell Peter, 'You know, I guess one person really can make a difference... Nuff said.'

Also rounding off a trio of cameos, long-time Sam Raimi cohort Bruce Campbell adds *Spider-Man 3*'s snotty maître d' to his Spidey résumé, which includes the wrestling announcer and rude theatre usher from the first and second films.

In a recent example of comic-book retconning gone awry, Marvel Comics have altered Spider-Man's past in the highly controversial series *One More Day*. As a result, the last 20 or so years of Spider-Man stories have been wiped from the character's history, including Peter's marriage to Mary Jane and the death of Harry Osborn, who has now 'returned from Europe'.

What the critics said: 'Oh, what a tangled web does *Spider-Man 3* weave. Overly long and complicated, it's packed with crowd-pleasing moments and satisfactorily wraps up the trilogy –

without quite capturing the magic of the first two instalments.'
Lou Lumenick, *New York Post*

'In an era of cynical, cash-in sequels, *Spider-Man 3*, like its two predecessors, has a heartbeat that resonates just as strongly as its box office ka-ching.' Peter Travers, *Rolling Stone*

Superhero Archetype: Through the character of Eddie Brock, *Spider-Man 3* offers one of the clearest examples of the mirror villain in superhero movies. In the film, as in the comics, Brock is a rival photographer. However, in the comics, Brock is a physically domineering, middle-aged man, while the film amends the character to make him even more analogous with Tobey Maguire's Peter Parker. The movie's Brock, played by Topher Grace (an actor who could also fill the Peter Parker role), is a young photographer, physically similar to Peter. In a further revision, the film even has the two photographers share the same love interest in Gwen Stacy, further heightening their comparability.

Where these two characters diverge is in their reaction to the alien symbiote. Though initially tempted by the symbiote, Peter does not surrender to its alien control, rejecting it. However, Brock submits to the power of the suit, taking on the villainous role of Venom; indulging his whims and revelling in destruction and mayhem. Both characters, initially so alike, are set apart by this one decision, with Brock, through Venom, becoming Peter's darkest shadow.

Verdict: If the Spider-Man trilogy were a three-course meal then *Spider-Man 3* would be the most self-indulgent of desserts. Sam Raimi, his time at the table growing short, seems to have ordered everything on the menu. So for our cinematic delectation we get Spider-Man with a side of alien symbiote, love interests, both vintage red (MJ) and sparkling new white (platinum-blonde Gwen Stacy) and a mouth-watering, but difficult-to-fit-on-one-plate, three-villain combo.

To lay the blame for this over-indulgence solely on Sam Raimi is perhaps unfair. The preceding chapters demanded that Goblin Jr make an appearance, while Raimi, never a fan of Venom, clearly had the symbiote-dripping villain pushed upon him by the studio, with his long-time favourite Sandman remaining the director's only real extravagance. Given their own film, any one of these villains would have been a worthy foe for the webbed wonder. Venom and Sandman are expertly brought to the screen by the CGI wizards but the well-cast actors are left battling for screentime as often as they contend with Spider-Man. As a result, their characters are unable to reach the nefarious heights set by previous Spidey tormentors Doctor Octopus and the Green Goblin. Only James Franco's New Goblin manages to really put our hero through his paces. Benefiting from a three-film story arc, Franco ensures Harry's encounters with Peter have plenty of venom without the help of an alien symbiote. It is one of the film's biggest disappointments that the most promising villain is relegated to sidekick status by the film's climax.

As for the hero himself, much was said prior to the release of the film that *Spider-Man 3* would explore Peter's dark side. To convey this, Raimi and his leading man Maguire take a risky, comical approach. So rather than brooding, dark Peter takes to wearing eyeliner as he sleazes his way down the streets of New York, stopping only to dance (badly) to impromptu jazz numbers. Though Maguire is clearly enjoying himself and the scenes are not without their charm, this further indulgence irrevocably fractures the film's reality. By pushing the story and its characters so far towards farce, it's unable to recover its credibility before what should have been an emotional climax. With an audience quite literally unsure whether to laugh or cry, the film's visually stunning finish is robbed of its dramatic heft. After two enjoyable early courses, the trilogy-closer leaves you feeling bloated.

Pow!Pow!Pow!

Vigilante Justice

In the closing moments of Richard Donner's *Superman,* as the Big Blue Boy Scout swoops down from the heavens to deliver Lex Luthor to prison, he pauses before leaving to assure the bewildered prison warden, 'We are all part of the same team.' But are they? Who deputised the Last Son of Krypton? Is it even possible to pin a badge on the Man of Steel? Superman is not part of the 'same team' as this awestruck lawman; he is not even part of the same species. Superman's alien ancestry has bestowed upon him god-like powers that place him beyond the laws of man. As such, his independent, unsanctioned actions are never questioned and certainly never categorised as vigilantism; a luxury not afforded to the equally heroic Batman, who cannot even take a leisurely drive in the Batmobile without prompting a full-scale police manhunt. Why are the similar, self-sacrificing actions of Batman branded as vigilantism, while his cloud-scraping contemporary is given free reign?

The caped crusader is not the only superhero vigilante; there are many heroes who have been branded with the superhero mark of Cain. Often they operate outside the law, like Daredevil and the Punisher. For some, the law, or at least its government, is their enemy, such as the terrorist V from *V for Vendetta,* while others such as Judge Dredd and RoboCop are lawmen in a system predicated on vigilantism. As Judge Dredd intones before passing final judgement on another hapless criminal, 'I am the Law.' Yet no superhero, from the previously mentioned Superman to Howard the Duck, has ever operated as part of the law, so why are the autonomous actions of these heroes cast in a different light?

One could argue that superheroes such as the Punisher and Daredevil are vigilantes because they kill their enemies. While this is true of many superhero vigilantes, it fails to consider how 'accepted' superheroes such as the Fantastic Four can clobber and burn Doctor Doom to little more than a hood ornament, as they do at the climax of *Fantastic Four*, without even a whisper of vigilantism.

No, it is something simpler than their actions that categorises these heroes as vigilantes. From ex-soldier the Punisher to the self-taught avenger Batman, these 'vigilantes' are very much human. Their actions, however selfless and heroic, are the actions of men operating outside the law. Even those vigilantes who possess powers, such as the cyborg RoboCop or the hyper-sensitive Daredevil, have more 'grounded' abilities than that of the high-swinging, planet-hopping variety typified by Spider-Man and Superman. The super-powered superhero is deified and thus held above man's law, while the hero motivated by and prone to human emotion and frailties is one of us, acting for us, but without our consent, and for this he is a vigilante.

If vigilantes are seen as ordinary humans, then they are vulnerable to human weaknesses such as pride, lust and revenge. This calls into question the motives of the hero, questions never asked of the irreproachable Superman or the amiable scientists of the Fantastic Four. Is their quest motivated by a need for justice or is it self-satisfying revenge? Bruce Wayne dedicated himself to becoming Batman to exact his vengeance on the nameless criminals that populate Gotham's seedy underbelly. But, could it be that the benefits to Gotham's law-abiding masses from Batman's never-ending quest are merely a by-product of his primary goal: to quell the rage that burns inside him? This concern did not hinder Tim Burton's Batman, who killed not only his nemeses, the Joker and the Penguin, but also their henchmen. However, the idea of vigilantism was a central concern of the more comic-book faithful *Batman Begins*. This is evident in the film where attorney Rachel Dawes reminds Bruce, 'Justice is about harmony, revenge is about you making yourself feel better,' and Alfred impresses on Batman that, 'It can't be personal or you're just a vigilante.' These questions are asked by the heroes' closest allies because of the personal traumas that mark their origins. With the exception of Spider-Man, no hero's origin is as cloaked in personal loss as the vigilante heroes. Superman may have lost his entire home planet, but as an infant he was too young to remember, and landing on Earth he was raised by the most caring adoptive parents a fledgling hero could hope for. In stark contrast, Batman was orphaned when his parents were shot before his eyes in an unnecessary act of greed and cowardice. Similarly, the X-Men may be isolated from society but at least they are together in an opulent mansion, while V is driven underground with only the detritus of his former life for company.

Many of these heroes are initially motivated by blind rage, which prompts their vigilantism, but as this anger is quelled they become temperate avengers, entering into an uneasy truce with the law. In *Batman Begins*, Batman's unwillingness to pass final judgement on these criminals prevents him from becoming consumed by vengeance. Daredevil, too, faces this conflict. He starts out as a death-dealing vigilante, but events motivate him to remember, 'I'm not the bad guy,' ultimately choosing to spare the Kingpin's life rather than give himself over to revenge. By moving from self-motivated rage to justice, even of the vigilante variety, the heroes are given the implicit approval of law and society, as seen by policeman Jim Gordon adopting the Bat-Signal at the end of both *Batman* and *Batman Begins*, and investigative reporter Ben Urich's encouraging words, 'Go get them Matt,' in *Daredevil*'s closing moments.

It remains one of the great ironies in superhero movies that if power corrupts, it is the powerless heroes who prove the most corrupting. Turning the axiom on its head, we see how the power-bereft hero V prompts city-wide vigilantism and revolt in *V for Vendetta*, and Lieutenant Gordon warns Batman of 'escalation', a response in the criminal fraternity to his brand of theatricality, simply signalled in *Batman Begins*' coda by a Joker playing card. Perhaps, while the exploits of supermen are beyond the reach of regular people, the example of an ordinary man engaged in extraordinary feats is an easier act to follow, bringing out the 'super' in us all.

RoboCop (1987)

Cast: Peter Weller (RoboCop/Alex Murphy), Nancy Allen (Anne Lewis), Dan O'Herlihy (The Old Man), Ronny Cox (Dick Jones), Kurtwood Smith (Clarence Boddicker), Miguel Ferrer (Bob Morton), Robert DoQui (Sergeant Warren Reed)

Crew: Paul Verhoeven (Director), Edward Neumeier and Michael Miner (Co-Writers), Sol Negrin and Jost Vacano (Directors of Photography), Frank J Urioste (Editor), Basil Poledouris (Score)

Created by: Edward Neumeier and Michael Miner

Plot: Across the television sets of Detroit, advertisements for replacement organs and other consumer products interrupt grim news delivered in an upbeat fashion by prosaic anchors; there is an imminent threat of nuclear war in Africa, and closer to home conglomerate OCP has just acquired control of Detroit's recently privatised police force. OCP needs to rid the city of crime before it can build a new utopian metropolis, Delta City, on Detroit's ruins. At a board meeting, second-in-command Dick Jones unveils 'the future of law enforcement', the robot ED 209, to the head of the company, the 'Old Man'. However, the robot malfunctions, killing a young employee. Bob Morton, an ambitious board member, seizes this opportunity to pitch his idea for a more reliable, cyborg cop to the Old Man, who gives him the greenlight, much to Jones' chagrin.

As part of OCP's efforts to curb crime, police officer Alex Murphy has been reassigned to the dangerous Metro West precinct. Murphy hits the streets with his new partner Anne Lewis, and the pair is soon in pursuit of a gang led by notorious cop-killer Boddicker. Murphy and Lewis track the gang to an abandoned warehouse where, out-numbered, Murphy is killed by the gang in a hail of gunfire. Clinically dead, Murphy is now property of OCP, who replace his tissue with cybernetics, making him RoboCop.

RoboCop begins a one-man war against crime with no memory of his former life as Murphy. But after seeing a member of Boddicker's gang, RoboCop begins to remember his old life. On regaining his memory, RoboCop arrests Boddicker and his gang. Boddicker tells RoboCop that he works for Dick Jones and that he will be back on the street in no time. RoboCop tries to apprehend Jones but a classified part of his programming, Directive 4, prevents him from arresting any OCP executive and renders him motionless. Jones tries to have ED 209 destroy RoboCop but he escapes with the aid of Lewis.

Fearing the implicating evidence in RoboCop's programming, Jones has Boddicker's gang released from prison and tasks them with destroying RoboCop. They track RoboCop down, but he and Lewis, though both gravely wounded, manage to defend themselves against Boddicker's gang, with RoboCop delivering a killer blow to Boddicker. With Boddicker out of his way, RoboCop takes out Jones' other protector ED 209, before barging into OCP's boardroom and playing the incriminating recording for the Old Man. A panicked Jones tries to take the Old Man hostage, with Directive 4 preventing RoboCop from intervening. But the Old Man fires Jones, which enables RoboCop to shoot him. As RoboCop holsters his gun the Old Man asks him his name, to which he confidently responds, 'Murphy.'

Trivia: Actor Miguel Ferrer who plays the cocaine-snorting OCP executive Bob Morton in *RoboCop*, is the son of *White Christmas* star Rosemary Clooney and former Batman George Clooney's cousin.

In the scene where RoboCop stops a convenience-store robbery, an Iron Man comic can be seen on the shelves. Iron Man, and its story of industrialist Tony Stark, who uses armour both to stay alive and as a weapon, was an influence on *RoboCop*.

Many of *RoboCop*'s supporting cast have lent their vocal talents to superhero television shows including Kurtwood Smith (*Justice League*, *Batman Beyond* and *Spawn*), Ray Wise (*Superman: Doomsday*) and Ronny Cox (*Spawn*). But it is Miguel Ferrer who has the most super-powered résumé, first playing the villain Weatherman in the ill-fated pilot for a live-action Justice League television series, then voicing another meteorology-themed villain, Weather Wizard, in *Superman: The Animated Series*, and most recently he provided the voice of the Martian Manhunter in *Justice League: The New Frontier*.

What the critics said: [Verhoeven's] cold, slick, funny, high-powered movie is informed by a humanism this genre almost always abandons in its chase after vigilante splat.' Jay Carr, *Boston Globe*

'The love of mayhem combined with a biting comic attack on neo-fascist corporatism… helped raise *RoboCop* above the common sci-fi herd.' Clark Collis, *Empire*

Superhero Archetype: RoboCop as a machine/man hybrid is often considered a science fiction hero first, but with a square jaw – the only glimmer of humanity visible beneath his armour – he fights for Truth and Justice in an America that has lost its way, proving that there is nothing artificial about his superhero archetype. Like all superheroes, the way RoboCop conforms to this archetype is indicative of the era in which he was created, with every aspect of the hero given a 1980s American overhaul.

RoboCop's origin contains the emotional trauma present in other superheroes, but is compounded by a physical degradation, his crucifixion by gunfire making his heroic resurrection resonate in a decade of muscle-bound heroes such as Conan the Barbarian and John Rambo. In another superhero motif, this origin also occurs at the hands of the villain who RoboCop must face in the film's climax.

The manner in which RoboCop's actions are licensed by the people of the city is somewhat atypical. As a cop he is programmed to protect and serve, but his programming is the dictum of a conglomerate more interested in profit margins than public trust. Only when he rejects his programming, rediscovering the identity that was secret even to himself, does he become a true hero and, ironically, also a vigilante.

Verdict: In 1987, as Superman took a much-needed break from superhero movies following the disappointment of *Superman IV*, a new Man of Steel rose to the screen, born not from the pages of a comic, but from the social unrest and crippling consumerism of 1980s America. *RoboCop* presented a near-future United States that was the realisation of the *Wall Street* maxim, 'Greed is Good', with the eponymous hero a blue collar and steel cowboy tasked with cleaning up Old Detroit with only his trusty sidearm for company. The film was Dutch director Paul Verhoeven's second American effort and he brought an outsider's perspective that critiqued the United States' privatisation and militarisation of the public sector.

This integration of social satire within the fabric of a superhero movie was not the only novel aspect of the film. *RoboCop* was the first addition to the genre that had not been adapted from a comic-book source. Yet it is still clad in comic-book armour, owing much to the hyper-stylised and often violent comics of the 1980s such as Judge Dredd and the work of Frank Miller (who would write the screenplay for the two *RoboCop* sequels).

The success of the film, like the cyborg himself, is due to its many parts working fluidly together. On the human side, Peter Weller animates his cyborg with sharp, bird-like movements, maintaining a surface coldness whilst hinting at the humanity beneath. The rest of the cast of yuppies, crooks and cops are fleshed out by reliable character actors, including Miguel Ferrer, Kurtwood Smith and Paul McCrane, who bring personality to their stock types. The script is embedded with sarcastic humour, which is at its most arid during the television clips of newscasters trying to deliver grave news through permanent grins, only to be constantly interrupted by advertisements and inane catchphrase comedies (a motif that recurs in Verhoeven's *Starship Troopers*).

On the artificial front, the practical special effects and stop-motion work hold up surprisingly well given how quickly many of today's digital effects age, while the music, a fitting blend of synthesisers and orchestral work, achieves a grander scale than the film's modest budget would allow in other areas. Yet in the end, *RoboCop* remains the director's film with Verhoeven's vision of a totalitarian consumer-driven society laughable in its excess, and chilling in its familiarity. Without Verhoeven on board for the sequels, neither the series nor, arguably, the director would ever reach the same heights again.

Pow!Pow!Pow!Pow!

Batman (1989)

Cast: Michael Keaton (Batman/Bruce Wayne), Jack Nicholson (The Joker/Jack Napier), Kim Basinger (Vicki Vale), Robert Wuhl (Alexander Knox), Pat Hingle (Commissioner Jim Gordon), Billy Dee Williams (Harvey Dent), Michael Gough (Alfred Pennyworth), Jack Palance (Carl Grissom)

Crew: Tim Burton (Director), Sam Hamm (Story and Screenplay), Warren Skaaren (Screenplay), Roger Pratt (Director of Photography), Ray Lovejoy (Editor), Danny Elfman (Score)

Created by: Bob Kane and Bill Finger

Plot: After robbing a wealthy family, two crooks crouch on a Gotham City rooftop. One tells the other about 'The Bat', who preys on criminals, just as a dark figure appears above them. This mysterious shape attacks and beats the thugs, before hanging one from the rooftop edge with the simple warning, 'Tell your friends... I'm Batman.'

Gotham is a city awash with crime, with its well-meaning Police Commissioner, Jim Gordon, unable to stem the tide. The city's crime-lord, Carl Grissom, organises a raid on a chemical factory to be headed by his 'number one guy', Jack Napier. But the raid is a ruse, as Grissom is leading Jack, whom he rightly suspects of having an affair with his girlfriend, into a police ambush.

Meanwhile, at a party hosted by wealthy socialite Bruce Wayne, Gordon finds out about the attempted raid and leaves to intervene. Wayne eavesdrops on Gordon's conversation and he too moves to the scene in the guise of Batman. At the factory, a shoot-out occurs between the mobsters and the police. Batman aids the police and in the process confronts Napier, whom during the course of their altercation, is inadvertently sent into a toxic bath and left for dead. But Napier is not dead, rather transformed by the chemicals into a creature with white skin, green hair and a permanent smile. Now calling himself the Joker, he kills Grissom and takes control of the mob family.

The Joker begins to pollute the city's consumer products with a fatal poison that leaves a smile transfixed on its victim's faces. He also takes an interest in photojournalist Vicki Vale, who has begun a relationship with Batman's alter-ego Bruce Wayne. The Joker lures Vicki to a museum where he vainly attempts to romance her, at which point Batman arrives to save her. Batman tells Vicki he has discovered the secret of the Joker's poison, information she in turn makes public. This infuriates the Joker, who now plans to poison Gotham's residents with a toxic gas that will be released at the city's busy bicentennial party. However, once again Batman foils the Joker's plan. In retaliation, the Joker kidnaps Vicki and takes her to the top of an abandoned cathedral. Batman battles through the Joker's henchmen, before facing the villain on the rooftop. But the Joker gains the upper hand, leaving Batman and Vicki hanging from the building. As the Joker boards a helicopter to escape, Batman throws a rope, tying the fleeing villain to a stone gargoyle. Unable to break free, the Joker slips to his death, while Batman manages to save himself and Vicki. The city, initially wary of Batman, now appreciates his help and he provides them with a means of reaching him should they ever need him again. Gordon tests this signal, a bright Bat emblem that shines into the sky, as Batman stands vigil on a rooftop: protector of the city.

Trivia: The role of District Attorney Harvey Dent in *Batman* is played by *Star Wars* actor, Billy Dee Williams. A scarred Dent, known as the villain Two-Face, was later played by Tommy Lee Jones in *Batman Forever*, and the character is set to reappear in the upcoming *The Dark Knight*, with the part to be played by Aaron Eckhart.

The release of *Batman* prompted the British Censorship Board to create a new rating standard '12', which would prevent younger children from seeing the somewhat violent film.

Batman would be regular Tim Burton-composer Danny Elfman's first superhero movie score. Elfman has since composed music for superhero movies *Darkman, Spider-Man, Hulk,* the upcoming *Hellboy II: The Golden Army*, and the comic book-based *Dick Tracy, Men in Black* and *Wanted*. He also scored the theme for the short-lived superhero television series *The Flash*, while his Batman theme would later be re-used in the excellent *Batman: The Animated Series*.

What the critics said: 'The wit is all pictorial, the film meanders mindlessly from one image to the next, as does a comic book.' Vincent Canby, *New York Times*

'Tim Burton's powerfully glamorous comic-book epic, with sets angled and lighted like film noir, goes beyond pulp. It has a funky, nihilistic charge, and an eerie, poetic intensity.' Pauline Kael, *The New Yorker*

Superhero Archetype: If Superman can be credited with the creation of the superhero archetype, then Batman should be recognised for its refinement. The clearest example of where the Gotham brand is more succinct than the Kryptonian model is in Batman's definite heroic impulse. Signalled by two gunshots, the murder of Bruce Wayne's parents forms the basis of Batman's archetype, and is the clear motivation for everything else that follows. This stands in sharp contrast to Superman's more muddled and ambiguous motivations of Truth, Justice and the American Way.

Further fine-tuning would be provided to the Dark Knight's archetype by *Batman*, where the relationship of hero to villain, a central tenet of the superhero archetype, is made more concise, and as a result more intense, allowing for a cyclical cinematic narrative. This amendment would see the identity of Bruce Wayne's parents' killer changed from the lowlife Joe Chill, as in the comics, to his antithetical villain Jack Napier; the clown prince of crime in his formative years. In doing so, the Joker becomes directly responsible for the origin of Batman, just as years later Batman plays a part in the Joker's birth. As Batman summarises in the film's climax, 'I made you, you made me first.'

Cinematic revisions, where the criminal who murdered a parent is revealed to be the adult hero's nemesis, have occurred in superhero movies since *Batman* was released. Examples include the Kingpin's murder of Daredevil's father and the revelation of Sandman's responsibility for Uncle Ben's death in *Spider-Man 3*. So, in the same way the comic-book Batman more tightly structured the superhero archetype, *Batman* sharpened the superhero archetype of the movies.

Verdict: Following the success of *Superman* in 1978, one would have expected other superheroes to ride that red-and-blue streak into the cinema. Yet the opposite occurred, with a superhuman drought persisting until 1989 when Tim Burton's *Batman* proved to be the wellspring from which others would later flow (*The Shadow, The Crow, The Phantom*). Batman's slow ascendance to the screen is in part attributable to the Adam West television series of

73

the 1960s, which itself had a spin-off feature. West's pop-art portrayal of Batman, though largely derided today, was a loving pastiche that capitalised on the aesthetic sensibilities of the era, while being much closer in tone to the comic-book Batman of the time than purists would like to remember. But this Technicolor caped crusader was now at odds with the more serious approach of *Superman* and the darker Frank Miller-led stories of the comics. The eventual film would be a dark and pulpy superhero movie drenched in film noir, which banished any lingering memories of camp, and brought the Dark back to the Knight.

Following the success of *Beetlejuice,* Tim Burton recalled the film's star Michael Keaton to play the dual roles of Batman and billionaire Bruce Wayne. The decision to cast an actor largely known for his comedic roles was met with angry outbursts from fans, but Keaton turned in an assured performance touched by an underlying psychosis, befitting these fractured parts. However, this Batman would not only be a change from the series, but also the comics; covered in rubber muscles and utilising an arsenal of gadgets, he was not unwilling to kill the criminal denizens of Gotham. While Batman may have had all the best toys, it would be the Joker who would get all the best lines, scenes, and even top billing; unsurprising given that Jack Nicholson was chosen to provide the clown prince of crime's grimace, a move that allayed many a fanboy's fears. Nicholson played the Joker as an exaggerated pale-faced version of his own persona, which broadly fitted the character, but on re-analysis the performance lacks any real depth. On love-interest duties, Kim Basinger effectively channelled the spirit of a 1950s femme fatale that would later serve her so well in *LA Confidential*, in a largely thankless role.

The film's greatest success would be its visual zeal. Not yet fully utilising the gothic fairytale aesthetic that would become his trademark, Burton fitted Gotham and its inhabitants out in a pulpy, 1950s style dotted by garish colour – each scene containing a sickly purple or toxic green. The film also contains many iconic moments such as the Bat-Plane silhouetted by the moon and the Joker's post-acid bath trip to the doctors, and the line, 'Have you ever danced with the devil by the pale moonlight.' But despite strong performances and bold visuals, the film is less than the sum of its parts, mired by weak action sequences that culminate with the young Batman beating the middle-aged Joker on a Gotham rooftop. It's to be commended for redeeming the Dark Knight, but what made it the most successful film of 1989 has been somewhat dimmed by the more Burtonesque sequel, and comic-book faithful *Batman Begins*. The best was yet to come.

Pow!Pow!Pow!

Daredevil (2003)

Cast: Ben Affleck (Daredevil/Matt Murdock), Jennifer Garner (Elektra Natchios), Colin Farrell (Bullseye), Michael Clarke Duncan (Kingpin/Wilson Fisk), Jon Favreau (Foggy Nelson), Joe Pantoliano (Ben Urich), David Keith (Jack Murdock)

Crew: Mark Steven Johnson (Director/Writer), Ericson Core (Director of Photography), Armen Minasian and Dennis Virkler (Co-Editors), Graeme Revell (Score)

Created by: Stan Lee and Bill Everett

Plot: Matt Murdock is a quiet kid living in one of New York's toughest neighbourhoods, Hell's Kitchen, with his father, the past-his-prime boxer 'Battling Jack' Murdock. One day, Matt sees his father working as a mob enforcer using strong-arm tactics to extort overdue money. Shocked, Matt tries to run from the scene, but an accident occurs when a forklift crashes against some barrels, spraying radioactive biohazard in Matt's face, blinding him. A guilt-ridden Jack vows to get his life back on track for his son, and returns to boxing. Meanwhile, as a result of his radioactive exposure, Matt's other senses become heightened to supernatural levels and he also develops a radar sense. Things soon improve for father and son, as Jack wins a number of matches and Matt develops his new powers. But when Jack refuses the mob's demands to throw his next fight, he is killed by an unseen mob enforcer.

Years later, the adult Matt Murdock is a lawyer struggling to convict the city's criminals. However, Matt's courtroom efforts are in vain, as the city's criminal Kingpin keeps his men out of prison. At night, in the guise of the vigilante Daredevil and aided by his heightened senses, Matt punishes those that the law cannot. Meanwhile, the Kingpin hires psychotic Irish assassin Bullseye to kill his former accomplice Nikolas Natchios. Natchios' daughter Elektra has begun a relationship with Matt, and, while attending a party with her, Matt discovers the Kingpin's plan, and as Daredevil moves to defend Natchios. As Natchios tries to escape the city with Elektra, he is attacked by Bullseye. Daredevil intervenes, but Bullseye manages to kill Natchios using Daredevil's billy-club. Elektra finds the billy-club, and, believing Daredevil to be her father's killer, plans to meet him in battle.

Elektra's hunt for Daredevil culminates in the two fighting on the city's rooftops. Unable to fight the woman he loves, Daredevil is severely wounded, leaving Elektra to unmask him. Elektra realises her mistake just as Bullseye reappears, and, with Daredevil wounded, she is forced to fight him alone. Elektra is no match for the master assassin, who kills her with one of her own sais. Daredevil, only barely recovered, fights Bullseye in a church and eventually wins, throwing him through a stained-glass window. Although wounded, Daredevil goes to the source of the city's criminality, attacking the Kingpin at his headquarters. Daredevil eventually wins the fight, but is unmasked in the process. Not wanting to be 'the bad guy', Daredevil allows him to be taken by the police rather than pass judgement. Though Kingpin is defeated, Matt continues his war against crime as Daredevil, the Man without Fear.

Trivia: Kevin Smith, writer/director of *Clerks* and *Chasing*

Amy, who cameos in the film as morgue worker Jack Kirby (a nod to the legendary comic-book artist), wrote the first eight issues for the re-launched Daredevil comic in 1998. The story-line, *Guardian Devil*, though successful in raising the profile and sales of the character's title, was controversial among fans for killing long-time Matt Murdock love interest, Karen Paige. The character of Karen briefly appears in *Daredevil* played by future *Grey's Anatomy* star Ellen Pompeo.

Jon Favreau, who portrays Matt Murdock's bumbling partner Foggy Nelson, is the director of new superhero movie *Iron Man*.

A director's cut of *Daredevil* is now available on DVD, which includes an entire subplot featuring rapper Coolio that was cut from the theatrical release.

What the critics said: 'As drawn from the Marvel Comics character... Daredevil, in this movie at least, is little more than a hollow clone of Batman and Spider-Man.' Owen Gleiberman, *Entertainment Weekly*

'But the real star here is that loveable Irish gobshite Colin Farrell, who mugs the movie... with his shameless, over-the-OTT performance as ultra-lethal hitman Bullseye.' Dan Jolin, *Total Film*

Superhero Archetype: Fittingly for a superhero without sight, Daredevil blindly follows the superhero archetype. From his responsibility borne of suffering (his father's murder) to the alliteration of alter-ego Matt Murdock's name, all the conventions of the superhero are present and correct. But where the film – directly drawing from the Frank Miller-written comics – enhances this archetype is in providing a love interest who is not only there to be saved. Elektra is a resilient, independent woman; a force to be reckoned with. It is little wonder why to date she joins Catwoman as the only superhero love interest to receive her own spin-off film. Despite the patchy quality of these features, it is still a more tempting prospect than two hours of Lois Lane's pining or Mary Jane's constant need to be saved.

Verdict: Prior to his revitalisation of the Batman comics, Frank Miller brought credibility and maturity, not to mention sales, to Marvel Comics' second-tier hero, Daredevil. During his early 1980s run on the character, first as artist and later as writer/artist, he introduced characters that challenged the hero both physically and emotionally. Chief among these was Elektra, a love interest who was Daredevil's equal, and not the kind of damsel-in-distress that marked his early years. Miller also made Bullseye a more central villain, increasing his prominence and menace, while 'borrowing' the Spider-Man villain Kingpin to become Daredevil's arch-nemesis. So when it came to adapting Daredevil to the screen, it was only logical for writer/director Mark Steven Johnson to start with the Miller years. However, where more recent Miller adaptations such as *Sin City* and *300* have maintained the author's blood-soaked edge, in fastening his narrative to a teen-friendly film – replete with a *du jour* alt-rock soundtrack – the film attenuates Miller's complexity and results in a muddled mix.

In the dual role of Daredevil/Matt Murdock, Ben Affleck fares well and Jennifer Garner summons the physicality perfected over years on her hit show *Alias* to effectively realise ninja Elektra. But it is Colin Farrell's scenery-chewing turn as Bullseye that steals the show; he invests each scene with such a volatile energy that his absence from the screen often leaves the film feeling flat.

The action sequences too are well handled, even if it is never fully explained how Daredevil's heightened senses allow him to jump from building to building with wild abandon, incurring little in the way of bodily injuries. Where the film falls apart is during the character-building scenes, as trite dialogue and cinema clichés (a love scene in front of a roaring fire?) try the audience's patience. The film also suffers from a Kingpin-sized hole, as Michael Clarke Duncan's meagre screentime sees him posture and puff large cigars but never convinces us that he is the city's all-powerful criminal mastermind. While *Daredevil* remains a worthwhile entrant to the superhero-movie canon, its below-par characterisation and dulled edge fail to give the Devil his due.

Pow!Pow!Pow!

Batman Begins (2005)

Cast: Christian Bale (Batman/Bruce Wayne), Michael Caine (Alfred), Liam Neeson (Ra's Al Ghul/Henri Ducard), Katie Holmes (Rachel Dawes), Gary Oldman (Lieutenant Jim Gordon), Cillian Murphy (Scarecrow/Dr Jonathan Crane), Tom Wilkinson (Carmine Falcone)

Crew: Christopher Nolan (Director/Screenplay), David S Goyer (Story/Screenplay) Wally Pfister (Director of Photography), Lee Smith (Editor), James Newton Howard and Hans Zimmer (Score)

Created by: Bob Kane and Bill Finger

Plot: When his wealthy parents are gunned down before his eyes by a random Gotham criminal, the orphaned Bruce Wayne sets about exacting revenge, 'to turn fear against those who would prey on the fearful'. In pursuit of his goal, Wayne travels the world learning from the criminal fraternity, and also how to fight them. His journey takes him to the mountain-top home of Ra's Al Ghul, where he learns 'theatricality and deception' at the hands of Al Ghul's accomplice, Henri Ducard. Upon completing his training, Wayne is asked by Al Ghul to lead his army in wiping out the 'beyond-saving' Gotham City. Wayne refuses, destroying Al Ghul's home and seemingly Al Ghul in the process.

On returning to Gotham, and reunited with his former butler and surrogate family Alfred, Wayne begins a double life. By day he is the boorish playboy Bruce Wayne, by night Gotham City's nocturnal protector the Batman. He is aided in his quest by the city's one decent cop Lieutenant Jim Gordon and Assistant

District Attorney Rachel Dawes, his childhood sweetheart. Wayne first takes down mob boss Carmine Falcone, and, chasing a lead from Falcone, discovers that drugs are being shipped into Gotham under the supervision of psychiatrist Dr Jonathan Crane. Batman learns that Crane, who also wears a mask and calls himself the Scarecrow, is in fact pouring a fear toxin into the city's water supply under the orders of an unnamed source. Batman confronts and defeats the Scarecrow, dousing him with his own fear toxin. The mastermind of the scheme soon reveals himself to Wayne to be his old teacher Ducard, who has in fact always been Ra's Al Ghul.

Al Ghul plans to destroy Gotham by dispersing the fear toxin from the city's water supply using a machine stolen from Wayne Enterprises. He begins to release the toxin, causing riots in the city; his final target is the city's water hub, which, if reached, will blanket the city in fear. Batman, aided by Gordon, moves to stop him. Batman tackles Al Ghul as he travels in a train with his toxin-dispersing machine; meanwhile, using the Batmobile, Gordon destroys the bridge on which the train is travelling. Batman escapes the train before it plunges from its tracks, but Al Ghul and his machine are destroyed. The city saved, Batman meets Gordon on the roof of police headquarters, where he is handed his next task, signalled by a single playing card – the Joker.

Trivia: Cillian Murphy was one of a number of actors, including Joshua Jackson, Billy Crudup, Hugh Dancy and Jake Gyllenhaal, who auditioned for the role of Batman. Director Christopher Nolan was so impressed with the actor's audition, he cast him as a Batman villain, alongside fellow Irishman Liam Neeson, who plays Ra's Al Ghul. Murphy will reprise the role of the Scarecrow in the upcoming *The Dark Knight*.

The scarred Arkham Asylum escapee Mr Zsasz, who is seen threatening Rachel Dawes with a knife during the film's climax, is played by Tim Booth, the frontman for Manchester band *James*.

The 2006 Forbes Fictional 15, which ranks the most affluent characters based on their wealth, places Bruce Wayne as the seventh richest fictional character with a net worth of approximately $6.8 billion, mainly derived from his inheritance. Wayne is one place ahead of the 'self-made' Tony Stark (Iron Man), who has a net worth of $3 billion; while Superman villain Lex Luthor, who was placed fourth on the 2005 list with a personal fortune of $10.1 billion, has mysteriously fallen off the most recent top 15, proving that crime doesn't pay.

What the critics said: '*Batman Begins* is, ultimately, an affectionate and stylish re-imagining of the Bob Kane comic books at its source, essentially serious and refreshingly free of camp.' Michael Dwyer, *The Irish Times*

'Scenes depicting the newly orphaned Bruce being comforted by a kindly cop or his steely determination to avenge their deaths as a teenager (an excellent Christian Bale in chilly *American Psycho* mode) give the superhero a rich sense of shading.' Edward Lawrenson, *Sight and Sound*

Superhero Archetype: With an extended rogues gallery, Batman has many villains who could be considered antithetical (the Joker) to his grim, pragmatic vigilantism, and others who mirror his traumatic past (Two-Face). In *Batman Begins*, the film uses villains little-known outside the comic world, but who brilliantly serve to mirror the hero's actions and the film's themes. Fittingly, Dr Jonathan Crane identifies himself as a Jungian psychiatrist while simultaneously personifying one of man's primal archetypes through his villainous alter-ego, the Scarecrow. Like Batman, the Scarecrow uses fear as a weapon, but where Batman uses it on those who prey on the fearful, the Scarecrow uses fear on anyone who gets in his way.

However, it is Ra's Al Ghul who presents the greatest parallels with Batman; both men are on a quest motivated by past losses and regard themselves as protectors. But while both are vigilantes,

Batman strives for justice rather than self-satisfying revenge, refusing to kill, stating 'I am no executioner', something Al Ghul considers 'necessary'. It is because of this decision that the two men, both so alike, are pitted against one another as adversaries. The film's effective use of this facet of the superhero archetype, of the hero and his darkest shadows, enriches the film's overall themes of fear, justice and revenge.

Verdict: Emerging from the Batcave after an eight-year cinematic hibernation that was forced upon the Batman by the dayglo excess of *Batman & Robin*, *Batman Begins* was always going to be a beast of a different nature. Grim and proper, and taking its cues from Frank Miller's landmark comic *Batman: Year One* in order to explore the origins of the Dark Knight, the film pushes its villains into the background. *Batman Begins* is the first Batman film to really be about Batman.

The story deals in painstaking detail with how Bruce Wayne went from orphan to relentless avenger. This makes for a compelling first act as the 'lost' Wayne learns theatricality and deception at the hands of Henri Ducard/Ra's Al Ghul on snow-capped mountains. However, the approach threatens to become laborious when Wayne dons the cape and cowl, and, almost embarrassed by its superhero status, the film seems compelled to explain and justify its high-flying indulgences at every turn. Thus, we finally see how Batman got his wonderful toys – borrowing the Batmobile, crash-testing his helmet and sharpening his Batarangs – with all the excitement of a DIY documentary. Fortunately, some excellent villains turn up to entice Batman out from his cave and give him something to fling his Batarangs at.

Cillian Murphy gives as menacing a performance *sans* mask as he does in the full Scarecrow garb, while Neeson's unveiling as the criminal mastermind is deftly handled and nicely timed. However, unlike Burton's *Batman*, the film remains the caped crusader's show, with Christian Bale proving a solid anchor for this origin story. The Welshman manages to infuse both Bruce Wayne and Batman with distinct identities; the former laced with shades of his earlier performance as *American Psycho*'s Patrick Bateman and the latter with a shouty, gravel-toned menace.

The film's climax delivers fantastic mayhem as Ra's Al Ghul's machinations see the demented residents of Arkham Asylum spill out onto the streets of Gotham, with the young Batman struggling to keep up. However, the real excitement is saved for the closing moments when, crisis averted, Batman meets Gordon by the newly installed Bat-Signal. A new villain is revealed to be in town, signalled by a Joker playing card; Batman has only begun.

Pow!Pow!Pow!Pow!

V for Vendetta (2005)

Cast: Hugo Weaving (V), Natalie Portman (Evey), Stephen Rea (Inspector Finch), Stephen Fry (Deitrich), John Hurt (Adam Sutler), Tim Pigott-Smith (Creedy), Sinéad Cusack (Delia Surridge)

Crew: James McTeigue (Director), Andy Wachowski and Larry Wachowski (Screenplay), Adrian Biddle (Director of Photography), Martin Walsh (Editor), Dario Marianelli (Score)

Created by: Alan Moore and David Lloyd

Plot: In a dystopian Britain, a young woman, Evey, is stopped by enforcers of the oppressive government who clearly have more than escorting her on their minds. But Evey is saved by V, a knife-wielding vigilante wearing a Guy Fawkes mask. V takes Evey to a rooftop, where, to the strains of Tchaikovsky's *1812 Overture,* he sets off an explosion that destroys the Old Bailey, leaving his tell-tale V symbol in the sky. V continues his vendetta by killing a paedophilic bishop, a hate-mongering newscaster and a doctor, Delia Surridge. It is only before the doctor dies that V reveals the motive behind his actions: he was the sole survivor of a series of government experiments that left his body scarred. His vendetta is against those who were involved in the experiments and the ideology they represent.

V attempts to enlist Evey in his plans but she escapes and goes to stay with her old colleague, the popular television presenter Deitrich. But when Deitrich publicly criticises the regime's High Chancellor, his house is ransacked and he and Evey are taken. Evey wakes in a cell, and, over an immeasurable amount of time, is tortured, starved and has her head shaven. One day Evey notices her cell door ajar, and in the hallway she discovers that she has been in V's lair the whole time, and that the torture she has endured was not at the hands of the government, but rather V himself. This moment of realisation allows Evey to crystallise essential truths about herself, society and her place within it. Though Evey returns to 'normal' life, she understands V is on course to fully realise his vendetta.

V's campaign has nurtured the seeds of dissent growing in the community. His identity has become synonymous with defiance. V prepares the way for his final act by agreeing to meet high-ranking members of the regime. During this encounter a fight breaks out that leaves V wounded and the members of the regime dead. Evey meets V in the city's underground, which he has reconstructed to allow a train carrying explosives to travel beneath the Houses of Parliament. V subsequently dies and Evey moves his body onto the train sending him towards his final desti-nation. Overwhelming the soldiers, thousands of people flood into the areas surrounding the Houses of Parliament; as the clock strikes twelve, the buildings explode and V's vendetta is complete.

Trivia: Alan Moore, writer of the original *V for Vendetta* comic, decided to remove his name from any future films based on his work, including *V for Vendetta*, following the poor adaptations of his *From Hell* and *The League of Extraordinary Gentlemen* graphic novels. It remains to be seen if Moore will be credited on the upcoming *Watchmen*.

To tie in with the various Guy Fawkes-themed elements of the film, *V for Vendetta* was originally slated for a November 5 release in 2005 to coincide with the 400th anniversary of Guy Fawkes' Gunpowder Plot. This terrorist action was an unsuccessful attempt by a group of English Catholics to blow up the Houses of Parliament and end Protestant rule in the country.

English actor James Purefoy (Marc Antony from TV's *Rome*) was originally cast as V, before being replaced after filming had started by *The Matrix*'s Hugo Weaving. Purefoy will next be seen in new superhero movie, *Solomon Kane*, as the sixteenth-century hero.

What the critics said: 'It's been turned into a Bush-era parable by people too timid to set a political satire in their own country.' *V for Vendetta* writer Alan Moore speaking to *MTV News*

'It's a terrific film… if you enjoyed the original and can accept an adaptation that is different to its source material but equally as powerful, then you'll be as impressed as I was with it.' *V for Vendetta* artist David Lloyd speaking to *Newsarama.com*

Superhero Archetype: Though the character of V would consider himself a revolutionary, V meets all the tenets of the superhero archetype – V for Vendetta, more like V for Vigilante Hero. Among the many aspects of the superhero archetype that V exhibits is a power and responsibility tied to his opposing force, the fascist government, and an origin that also motivates his sidekick, Evey. But where V's archetype is most interesting is in its subversion of the superhero secret identity as brilliantly realised in Moore's original work, where several possible identities for V are hinted at, with Evey herself taking on the role following V's demise. So uncertain is V's identity in the graphic novel that even his corporality is in question, with only hazy *sans* costume viewings of V seen.

The film forgoes this ambiguity by giving us close-up shots of V's scarred, but clearly human, hands. However, the film does maintain the uncertainty of V's identity. Many possibilities are mooted, with Evey summarising, 'He was Edmond Dantés… and he was my father, and my mother... my brother... my friend. He was you... and me. He was all of us,' over shots of a crowd of Vs removing their masks to reveal the faces of all those who stood and fell in defiance of the government. As V in his own words puts it, 'Beneath this mask there is more than flesh. Beneath this mask there is an idea... and ideas are bulletproof,' and in the end V's secret identity remains just that: secret.

Verdict: When Alan Moore and David Lloyd's original comic book *V for Vendetta* was published in the 1980s, it served as an acerbic indictment of Thatcherism, as filtered through the superhero genre. Therefore, when it was announced that the graphic novel was to be adapted to the screen so soon after the big-screen sanitisation of another Moore work, *The League of Extraordinary Gentlemen*, fans of the four-colour polemic were understandably apprehensive. But the final film, scripted by *The Matrix* creators Larry and Andy Wachowski and directed by James McTeigue (First AD on the *Matrix* sequels), pleasantly surprised all but the most pedantic of fans. *V for Vendetta*, the film, does not dutifully follow its source material, preferring instead to contemporise dated concerns by alluding to every current socio-political hot potato from 'the American war' to 'avian flu'. The film also effectively condenses the graphic novel's 250-plus page count, while making some welcome amendments such as Stephen Fry's politically conscious talk-show host Deitrich – imagine Jonathan Ross if he presented *Newsnight*.

Surprisingly for a very British story, the two leads are played by an American and an Aussie. Embellished from the comics' cipher to a more confident woman, Evey is well realised by Portman, who effectively charts the character's emotional progression from V's captive to unwitting accomplice, and finally fellow revolutionary – even if she does struggle with the English accent. Weaving has no such vocal difficulty, with the actor who seethed menace in every halted syllable behind the shades of *The Matrix*'s Agent Smith managing to convey the playfully sardonic freedom fighter, despite being covered by a mask throughout. The rest of the cast of trusted British (John Hurt, Stephen Fry) and Irish (Stephen Rea, Sinéad Cusack) actors perform as their pedigree would suggest, with Fry deserving particular plaudits for one of his best screen performances yet.

Given *V for Vendetta*'s subject matter, the film came to the screen with little by way of controversy. Perhaps in today's climate the only mainstream film that could have a terrorist as a hero and avoid tabloid scorn would be a superhero movie, a genre often dismissed as being CGI-laden action spectacles. It is therefore ironic that the action sequences are the film's biggest letdown. While never poor, the climactic slow-mo finale feels too at odds with the rest of the film's rhetoric-heavy narrative. Effective in *The Matrix*, this bullet time – or knife time as it should be called here – is out of place in this less kinetic world; V deserves action with greater Verisimilitude. Though not as incendiary as the original work, the film's story remains the conflict of two opposing ideologies. Even if Moore's anarchy is tempered to big-screen democracy, the film, like the comic, succeeds in integrating socio-political examination into a gripping superhero tale.

Pow!Pow!Pow!Pow!

Family First

Superheroes are the rockstars of the multiplex. They dress with retro flair, keeping unsociable hours as they are adored by millions; a law unto themselves. Also, like musicians, most superheroes prefer to fly solo, while some are willing to share the spotlight. But how does a new hero go about forming a team? It is not as if they can put an ad in the personals: 'Wanted: like-minded meta-humans to join new superhero team. Kryptonite immunity preferable but not essential. Must have own bullet-proof costume and alliterative alter-ego. Influences include Batman, Green Lantern and the early work of the X-Men. Wonder Twins need not apply.' Even if you do assemble your own supergroup, you never know what's hiding behind your associate's mask. At any stage, one of your band of superbrothers could betray the team, or worse, upstage you with a solo project. Even with such potential calamities, if a hero still wanted to set up a club, they could do worse than look to the example of the Bee Gees, Jackson 5 and Hanson by keeping it in the family. If blood is thicker than water, than surely cosmic-irradiated mutant blood must have the reliable consistency of week-old jelly.

The Incredibles were the first superhero movie stars to make saving the world a family business, with Mr Incredible Bob Parr and his wife Elastigirl (née Helen) tackling the evil genius Syndrome with their super-powered kids in tow. *The Incredibles*, Pixar's excellent family comedy-cum-superhero adventure, follows Bob as he discovers that, although being married with children can tug on the cape of your heroic ambitions, when your back is to the wall saving the world can be a family affair.

Though they may not be a nuclear family like the Incredibles, the Fantastic Four are certainly nuclear-powered. Created in the 1960s, the Fantastic Four, particularly in their origin, articulated the anxiety felt by the average American family over the potential dangers presented by the rapid technological changes of the time. Reaching for the stars as scientists and explorers, the Fantastic Four fell to Earth as a family of gods. They might be giants but they are a family first, and as such they are party to all the squabbles and infighting of any family unit. The films updated the Fantastic Four origin but retained the family dynamic with Mr Fantastic and the Invisible Woman the de facto parents; the Thing the uncle/brother; and the Human Torch the attention-seeking child, with the sibling rivalry between Ben and Johnny most effectively rendered. However, the big-screen adaptations seem more interested in the family's celebrity status than the relationships between them, portraying the Fantastic Four as a super-star freakshow – like the Osbournes with powers.

While *Fantastic Four* joins *The Incredibles* in the superhero-movie canon as a crime-fighting clan, the latter, though animated (a form of filmmaking normally associated with children's entertainment), exhibits greater maturity, through its realistic portrayal of family life. The CGI success of *The Incredibles* may also have prompted another family to return to the screen. In 2007 the pseudo-superhero brothers, the Teenage Mutant Ninja Turtles, were coaxed out of their shells for a pixel-powered feature *TMNT*, with the CGI a natural fit for the anthropomorphic reptiles. Though clumsy in its realisation, the film comes to life during the moments of sibling rivalry between head of the clan Leonardo and the impetuous Raphael.

Like the modest success of *TMNT*, superhero families are at their best when they are exploring the relationships not found in other superhero teams such as X-Men and the Justice League of America. The members of the Fantastic Four and the Incredibles did not choose to be on the same team, but are bound by blood, and with this high-powered nepotism comes a recognisable family dynamic amidst the far-flung fantasy. In these superhero dynasties one finds marriages under super-strain and sibling rivalry with special powers, all while the characters are constantly reminded that you can choose your superfriends, but not your superfamily.

A recurrent trait in these heroic dynasties is how super-powers are often an extension of the hero's personality and role within the family. Fittingly, the pants-wearer in the Incredibles clan and the avuncular Thing of the Fantastic Four have super-strength; the speedster Dash and firestarter the Human Torch are the impulsive youths of their groups; and the leader Mr Fantastic and multi-tasking mother Elastigirl can be everywhere at once thanks to their stretchy special powers.

Despite the potential for high-powered domestics, there are benefits to coming from super-powered stock, as any orphaned vigilante will attest. While Spider-Man must engage villains with the fear of reprisals against his Aunt May or Mary Jane weighing on him, Mr Fantastic doesn't have to worry that anything will happen to his nearest and dearest, as they're right beside him facing down Doctor Doom or world devourer Galactus. That these superclans are still on speaking terms, while others end up in the divorce courts or on the therapist's couch, proves that nothing brings a family together like colour-coordinated suits and saving the world. The family that saves together, stays together.

The Incredibles (2004)

Cast: Craig T Nelson (Mr Incredible/Bob Parr), Holly Hunter (Elastigirl/Helen Parr), Jason Lee (Syndrome/Buddy Pine), Samuel L Jackson (Frozone/Lucius Best), Spencer Fox (Dashiell 'Dash' Parr), Sarah Vowell (Violet Parr), Brad Bird (Edna 'E' Mole)

Crew: Brad Bird (Writer/Director), Andrew Jimenez, Patrick Lin and Janet Lucroy (Directors of Photography),

Stephen Schaffer (Editor), Michael Giacchino (Score)

Created by: Brad Bird

Plot: Everyone's favourite superhero Mr Incredible is trying to make it to the church on time, stopping only to foil a bank robbery, team up with Elastigirl and save a cat from a tree. He is pestered throughout by his number one fan and wannabe side-kick, Buddy, who inadvertently causes a train to derail, requiring Mr Incredible to save the commuters. Mr Incredible chastises Buddy, reminding him he is not 'super', before arriving at the church in his civilian identity of Bob Parr to marry Helen (Elastigirl). But their wedded bliss is soon interrupted by a rise in public distrust of superheroes, which forces all costumed wonders to enter a government relocation scheme.

Fifteen years later, Bob is working a mindless office job while Helen is happy as a stay-at-home mom. They have three children: the shy teen Violet who can turn invisible, fourth-grader Dash who can run at imperceptible speeds and baby Jack-Jack who has yet to develop powers. Bob makes it through the day by listening to the police scanner with his old partner Frozone, waiting for an opportunity to save the world. The chance comes when Bob finds an electronic message from Mirage, a woman who offers Bob the job of stopping a robot gone awry on a secret island. Bob defeats the robot and continues to receive work from Mirage's mystery boss, but tells Helen he is away at work conferences. However, while on a new mission, Bob is attacked by his mystery benefactor, who is revealed to be the adult Buddy. The one-time fan has made his fortune designing inventions, which he has in turn used to become the 'Super' Syndrome.

Meanwhile, Helen discovers from their old supersuit-maker Edna that Bob is back in costume. She uses a homing device in Bob's suit to locate him, and now as Elastigirl flies to the island in a borrowed jet, with Violet and Dash having crept aboard. Though the jet is shot down, the three use their powers to make it safely to the island. Helen moves to save Bob while the children tackle

Syndrome's henchmen. Though finally reunited, the family's joy is short-lived as they are captured by Syndrome, who is now free to execute the next stage of his plan. He launches a rocket at the city with a robot onboard, which he plans to then stop, becoming a beloved hero. The family escape and pursue Syndrome, arriving in the city in time to stop the robot with the help of Frozone. Returning home, the family find Syndrome with Jack-Jack, whose chameleon-like powers manifest themselves, allowing him to escape the villain's grasp. Syndrome tries to flee in his airship but is dragged into its jets by his flapping cape. Three months later the family are attending Dash's track meet when a subterranean villain the Underminer attacks. Exchanging a knowing look, the family don their masks as the Incredibles.

Trivia: The Incredibles' pint-sized costume-maker Edna Mole is voiced by the film's writer/director, Brad Bird.

Jason Lee, who voices the villain Syndrome, played comic-book enthusiast Brodie in *Mallrats* and comic-book inker Banky in *Chasing Amy*, both of which were written and directed by some-time comic scribe Kevin Smith. In *Mallrats*, Lee's character Brodie meets another Lee, Stan, to discuss, amongst other things, the logistics of superhero sex organs.

Michael Kamen, who composed the score for superhero movie *X-Men* and Bird's *The Iron Giant*, was set to score *The Incredibles* before his death in 2003.

What the critics said: 'A spectacularly rendered tale of a family of superheroes, takes the art form to a whole new level.' Lou Lumenick, *New York Post*

'By building the family bond into the DNA of his story, Bird has crafted a film that doesn't ring cartoonish, it rings true.' Peter Travers, *Rolling Stone*

Superhero Archetype: Apart from a few talking heads and a night of pre-nuptial superheroics, *The Incredibles* gives little indication of what type of hero Bob Parr used to be before his enforced early retirement. We know that, like Daredevil and Batman, Bob was a hero who liked to mix business with pleasure, teaming up with superheroine Elastigirl for more than just crime-fighting. We also learn that Mr Incredible does not advocate sidekicks, dismissing future Syndrome Buddy's Incredi-Boy, and teaming up instead with Frozone, a cat too cool to be anyone's short-pants assistant. Yet most of Mr Incredible's early archetype remains a mystery.

One thing is for certain: as soon as Bob's family get in on the saving-the-world act, it is clear that the superhero archetype is in their genes. The Parrs are a family, but it is Syndrome's actions that bring them together as superheroes. This non-super villain, the opposite of the power-wielding Parrs, is directly responsible for the Incredibles' origin as a superhero unit, in the same way Mr Incredible, by his dismissal of Buddy's superhero ambitions, is responsible for Syndrome's. This adherence to the superhero archetypal tenet of the antithetical villain, whose origin is intertwined with that of the heroes, is not the only instance where the Incredibles exhibit time-tested superhero traits. Another superhero motif present in the first family of superherodom is how the Incredibles hide their gifts behind mundane, everyday personas, leading ineffectual lives, losing the races they could easily have won. By possessing an arch-nemesis and secret identities that contrast their own, Bob and Co make following the superhero archetype a family affair.

Verdict: With alliteration like Brad Bird, *The Incredibles'* director's name could easily be the *nom de plume* of any caped wonder, and based on the evidence of this superhero movie there is more than a hint of the superhuman to the animation auteur. For *The Incredibles,* Bird masterfully blended the idea of the superhero family, first seen in the pages of the *Fantastic Four,* into a post-*Watchmen* superverse of outlawed heroes. Bird earned his animation stripes on *The Simpsons*, and his own superclan tickle many of the same ribs as Homer and Co, but *The Incredibles* is much more than a super-Simpsons.

Opening during a Golden Age of superheroes, with Mr Incredible a full-service hero saving cats from trees and tackling ridiculously monikered villains such as Bomb Voyage, the film quickly moves into cold reality as this age gives way to rust. These suburban-set scenes, never a condemnation of family life – the one-time Elastigirl seen happy in her domesticity – criticise a society that requires conformity, where everyone is special so no one is.

Throughout the film, Pixar's animation is not just flawless, but fantastically malleable, with more visual inventiveness in a single frame than most superhero movies manage in their entire running time. It is not only the superheroes and their powers, brilliantly realised and deftly combined, that benefit from Pixar's pixel paintbrush, with every element of *The Incredibles'* retro-futuristic world lovingly created and carefully constructed, from Bob's tiny, grey cubicle to Syndrome's Blofeldian volcano lair.

As we have come to expect from Pixar, the vocal cast is pitch-perfect, with Craig T Nelson and Holly Hunter striking a genuine marital interplay, and the children actually sounding and talking like kids rather than self-conscious adults. However, it is Jason Lee who impresses most: stretching his vocal chords from the young Buddy to the adult Syndrome, he provides the necessary consistency to turn the superfan into an embittered villain.

With so many films trying to give their superhero stories an everyday realism at the expense of the fantastic, Pixar created a superhero movie of crime-fighters without capes, but who are nonetheless cloaked in the incredible.

POW!POW!POW!POW!POW!

Fantastic Four (2005)

Cast: Ioan Gruffudd (Reed Richards/Mr Fantastic), Jessica Alba (Sue Storm/The Invisible Woman), Chris Evans (Johnny Storm/The Human Torch), Michael Chiklis (Ben Grimm/The Thing), Julian McMahon (Victor von Doom), Kerry Washington (Alicia Masters), Laurie Holden (Debbie McIlvane)

Crew: Tim Story (Director), Mark Frost (Co-Writer), Michael France (Co-Writer), Oliver Wood (Director of Photography), William Hoy (Editor), John Ottman (Score)

Created by: Stan Lee and Jack Kirby

Plot: Brilliant but bankrupt scientist Reed Richards and his long-time friend Ben Grimm visit Reed's old classmate Victor von Doom. Reed convinces Doom, now a successful businessman, to let him use his space station to examine a mutagenic storm that will soon be travelling past Earth. Joining the crew of Reed, Ben and Doom is Sue Storm, Reed's ex-girlfriend, and her reckless pilot brother Johnny. Midway through the mission, the storm picks up pace, catching the team off-guard, forever altering their DNA and their lives.

On Earth, they begin to develop powers: Reed can stretch his body, Sue can turn invisible, Johnny becomes a Human Torch and Ben transforms into a rock-covered Thing. Distraught at his irreversible appearance Ben goes to the top of the Brooklyn Bridge, where he saves a man from jumping but inadvertently causes a dangerous pile-up. Reed, Sue and Johnny find Ben, and the foursome use their new powers to ensure that no one is hurt. Following the rescue, the media dub them the 'Fantastic Four'. In order to discover how to reverse their mutation, Reed takes them to his lab in the Baxter Building. Just as the Fantastic Four become media darlings, Doom's stock begins to plummet, and he too begins to change, with his skin becoming metallic. Blaming

Reed for his current woes, Doom plans to divide and conquer the Fantastic Four.

Doom first uses a machine Reed has been working on to reverse Ben's mutation. He also captures Reed before targeting the Baxter Building with a heat-seeking missile that Johnny, propelled by his flames, manages to lead away and destroy. Sue goes to save Reed but is overpowered by Doom. As they struggle, Ben, once more the Thing, arrives in time to clobber Doom. Their fight spills out onto the street, where Ben is soon aided by his team-mates. Leading the assault against Doom, Reed tells Johnny to superheat the metal-covered maniac while Sue contains the flames. Following the massive heat, Ben douses Doom with water from a fire hydrant, causing his body to contract, leaving him motionless. The Fantastic Four celebrate their victory with a party at which Ben tells Reed he is happy to stay as the Thing, and Reed proposes to Sue as Johnny burns a '4' into the sky. Appearing lifeless, Victor's hardened husk is shipped to the Eastern European nation of Latveria, but an electronic tremor suggests he may not be doomed to this dormant form.

Trivia: *Fantastic Four* co-creator Stan Lee, making his trademark cameo appearance, plays the heroes' kindly mailman, Willy Lumpkin. This marks the only time Lee, in a change from his previously anonymous roles, plays a character that has appeared in the comics. In the sequel, Lee's cameo at Reed and Sue's wedding is a nod to a scene from the original comic-book wedding, where Lee and *Fantastic Four* co-creator Jack Kirby tried to crash the wedding.

Among the various actors considered to play the Fantastic Four were Brendan Fraser (Mr Fantastic), James Gandolfini (The Thing), Paul Walker (The Human Torch) and Kate Bosworth and Rachel McAdams (The Invisible Woman).

What the critics said: 'More superhero sitcom than comic-book adventure... Though their powers may be super, these characters are way too self-involved to be heroic.' Kevin Crust, *Los Angeles Times*

'The really good superhero movies, like *Superman, Spider-Man 2* and *Batman Begins*, leave *Fantastic Four* so far behind that the movie should almost be ashamed to show itself in the same theatres.' Roger Ebert, *Chicago Sun-Times*

Superhero Archetype: As any worried web-spinner or suspicious Superman will tell you, being a superhero is a dangerous occupation. You never know when one of your old nemeses is going to seek vengeance by attacking your friends and family. One way to offset any collateral damage is to disguise your identity with a mask and descriptive *nom de plume*. Another is to ensure your nearest and dearest are as adept at derring-do as you, allowing you to forgo the cumbersome capes and secret identities.

The members of the Fantastic Four, while following a superhero archetype, fulfil the secret identity in name only. They use catchy monikers such as the Human Torch and Mr Fantastic to complete their superhero persona but don't rely on them to safeguard a secret identity as other heroes do. By having a superpowered family, they can flaunt their rocky, stretchy, fiery, invisible faces safe in the knowledge that their family members can handle any sort of reprisal.

Fantastic Four and its sequel explore the idea of the unmasked superhero, with the heroes becoming sought-after celebrities. The downside of this exposure is demonstrated through Reed and Sue – the Posh and Becks of superhero movies – proving in the sequel that stopping a megalomaniac doctor is nothing next to organising a celebrity wedding away from the prying eyes of the world's media. Such attention is not likely to trouble Peter Parker should he ever decide to make a decent woman out of MJ, one of the hidden benefits of being a hero with a mask.

Verdict: Following *The Incredibles* into the cinema, the characters that provided the inspiration for Pixar's heroes, the Fantastic Four, arrived on screen in the summer of 2005. However, this was not the superhero family's first attempt to crack the movie business, with a cheap, Roger Corman-produced version filmed in 1994 but never released. That attempt was crude, and a poor adaptation of Marvel Comics' first family, but, as this more recent effort proves, bigger budgets do not always mean better films.

Skewing younger, both in the characters' ages and the target audience, *Fantastic Four* presented itself as a light alternative to that summer's other superhero movie, the gloomy *Batman Begins*. However, in aiming to include the kids, the film feels free to rely on juvenile plotting and pre-school spectacle. What little story there is sees the Fantastic Four, now five with Victor von Doom in tow, heading to space to be imbued by cosmic radiation that awakens their elemental powers. However, many of these space travellers are miscast or poorly realised. Ioan Gruffudd has neither the necessary years nor big-screen presence to convince as the team's leader, while Jessica Alba's portrayal of the blonde-haired, blue-eyed 'Director of Genetic Research' is as transparent as her character's power. Furthermore, in what is probably the worst decision made in a superhero movie since Joel Schumacher thought the Batsuit would look better with nipples, Eastern European supervillain Doctor Doom is recast as the mincing head of a Fortune 500 company. On the plus side, Michael Chiklis is perfect as the ever-lovin', blue-eyed Thing, even if his costume is more rubber than rock. Yet even this character is mishandled, with Ben in a pathos-quashing move happily accepting his rocky exterior by the film's close. Surprisingly, it is the comic's least explored character that provides the brightest sparks, as Chris Evans' Human Torch appears to be the only one (audience included) enjoying this comical, comic-book movie.

The Torch also provides the movie's best action moments, with the larger sequences (of which there are only three) being lack-lustre at best. Apart from the necessary space mission, a bridge-bound pile-up caused by the Thing and a 'climax' in which the quartet gang up on Doctor Doom are lazily rendered. The sequel, *4: Rise of the Silver Surfer*, would improve on this original, concentrating on its most successful character the Human Torch, and having the cosmos–gliding hood ornament add some much–needed visual flair. However, the fundamental problems of the original remain, with poor casting and a wafer-light tone that values comedy montages over moments of drama or action. There may be a third *Fantastic Four* film, but in order to reach their eponymous number this superhero clan will have to improve on these tepid two.

Pow!Pow!

Strength in Numbers

Traditionally, cinema's superheroes have been a lonely breed; singular sentinels careering through the sky or lone avengers clinging to the shadows, returning at the end of each day to their respective fortresses of solitude. Even when companionship did find these masked men, it was more often in the form of an adolescent sidekick or cape-wearing canine than in the embrace of the larger superhero fraternity. Outside of the movies, superheroes have long learned the value of friendship; cartoons such as *Super Friends* saw Batman entering into a crime-fighting syndicate with Superman, Aquaman and even the Wonder Twins and their pet space-monkey Gleek, while Spider-Man, when attending Empire State University, was found cohabiting with the potentially volatile mix of Iceman and Firestar in *Spider-Man and his Amazing Friends*. Comics too have long fostered the fellowship of the super-powered with titles such as *All-Winners Squad*, *Justice League of America* and *The Avengers*, and it is from comics that the first successful superhero team, the *X-Men*, arrived on screen.*

Following the unexpected box-office popularity of *X-Men*, one could have been forgiven for anticipating squadrons of superhero teams to come cascading across the cinema screen. Instead, the success of *X-Men* facilitated the arrival of sole heroes such as Spider-Man and Daredevil, and allowed past masters

* Earlier entrant *Mystery Men* does not make the grade; apart from being unsuccessful, this weak satire follows a group of unapologetic super-zeros whose collective ineptitude would place them beneath space monkey Gleek and Krypto the Super Dog in the superhero pecking order.

Superman and Batman to return and begin again, with only the hyper-attenuated *League of Extraordinary Gentlemen* limply flying the flag for the superhero troupes. Perhaps cinema audiences find their heroes less heroic when they need to get by with a little help from their crime-fighting friends? More likely it comes down to numbers – not the number of heroes filling out the ranks of the latest team of intrepid defenders, but rather those printed on studio invoices. Why have ten heroes in one movie, when you can have ten movies each with a hero all of their own?

This power of one even made its way into superhero movies' first team, with the X-Men sequels kowtowing to the prevailing singular hero worship. While the original *X-Men* film benefited from a cast of little-known actors working cohesively in an ensemble piece, the post-*Van Helsing*, post-Oscar, post-*Lord of the Rings* success of actors Jackman, Berry and McKellen saw their characters begin to monopolise the focus of the sequels. Other characters, played by less famous faces, were soon marginalised (Cyclops), killed (Xavier, Cyclops), marginalised then killed (Cyclops again), killed then marginalised (Jean Grey), de-powered (Rogue) and completely forgotten (Nightcrawler), as the films pandered to their 'star' attractions. Continuing with this formula, one to which most superhero movies subscribe, the X-Men have now been disbanded so that Wolverine and Magneto may pursue their big-screen endeavours unencumbered by hangers-on.

While groups of heroes may be considered too cumbersome for the big screen, *Heroes* have found plenty of space on the small screen. The fantastically popular television show, which takes an *X-Men*-like approach to the idea of superheroes living among us, demonstrates how several can share the spotlight, from heroin-addicted clairvoyant painters to invulnerable cheerleaders. With its multi-episode format, television has always better facilitated superhero teams, from *Buffy the Vampire Slayer*'s ever-faithful Scoobies to *Smallville*'s Clark

Kent forming his own Junior Justice League with younger versions of the Green Arrow, Aquaman, the Flash and Cyborg.

However, following the disappointing box-office performance of Superman's return, DC Comics and Warner Bros are falling back on the old axiom of strength in numbers. Their next foray into superhero movies sees George Miller (*Mad Max*) working on a big-screen adaptation of *Justice League of America* (*JLA*), to include Batman and Superman alongside Wonder Woman, The Flash, Green Lantern and Aquaman. Does this mean a change in tactics of bigger being better? It is more likely that Warner Bros is putting all their super-eggs in one basket, hoping the resulting film will be fertile enough to harvest future series of individual heroes. The Justice League will also be joined on screen by the former *enfants terribles* of the superhero world, Watchmen, who are being brought to life by Zack Snyder, a man for whom a superhero team of six should be no problem, having already juggled *300*. Also, with crossovers between *Iron Man* and Hulk Mk II, the tantalising prospect of a big-screen version of Marvel supergroup *The Avengers* (not to be confused with the cult 60s spy series or the awful film that followed) seems ever closer. With *JLA* and *Watchmen* nearly upon us and *The Avengers* on the cinematic horizon, maybe audiences will soon discover that, when it comes to superheroes, one really is the loneliest number.

X-Men (2000)

Cast: Hugh Jackman (Wolverine/Logan), Patrick Stewart (Professor Charles Xavier), Ian McKellen (Magneto/Eric Lensherr), Famke Janssen (Jean Grey), James Marsden (Cyclops/Scott Summers), Halle Berry (Storm/Ororo Munroe), Anna Paquin (Rogue/Marie), Rebecca Romijn-Stamos (Mystique)

Crew: Bryan Singer (Director/Story), Tom DeSanto (Story), David Hayter (Screenplay), Newton Thomas Sigel (Director of Photography), Steven Rosenblum, Kevin Stitt and John Wright

(Co–Editors), Michael Kamen (Score)

Created by: Stan Lee and Jack Kirby

Plot: In the near future, a sub–species of humanity has evolved, developing strange new powers and abilities. These 'mutants' are feared and hated by the rest of mankind. One such mutant, Professor Charles Xavier, a wheelchair–bound telepathic pacifist, has opened a school for mutants where they can learn about their abilities so that they may integrate into society. The faculty of this school are the X–Men, former students, who now use their powers to defend humanity and teach young mutants. Meanwhile, Xavier's former ally, Magneto, now leads a band of terrorist mutants known as the Brotherhood, who feel mutants should take their place in society by any means necessary. Magneto's accomplice, Sabertooth, attacks two mutants – a life–force–sapping teen Rogue, and Wolverine, a loner with the ability to instantly heal from his wounds. They are rescued by the X–Men Cyclops and Storm, who bring them to their school.

Wolverine wakes in the strange surroundings of Xavier's establishment, with resident doctor and telepath Jean Grey tending to his wounds. The solitary mutant is asked by Xavier to stay with the X–Men. Meanwhile, another of Magneto's accomplices, the shape–shifter Mystique, infiltrates the school posing as a student. Mystique convinces Rogue to leave the school and also sabotages Xavier's power–enhancing machine Cerebro. Realising Rogue has left, the X–Men track her down at a train station, but when Magneto attacks they are unable to prevent Rogue from being captured. The X–Men return to the school as Senator Robert Kelly arrives. Kelly, a mutant–hating politician, has just escaped Magneto, who turned him into a mutant by using a machine powered from his magnetic abilities. Xavier tries to use Cerebro to track Rogue but Mystique's tampering renders him comatose. Jean repairs Cerebro and discovers that Rogue is being held by the Brotherhood at Liberty Island. The X–Men deduce that Magneto is planning to pass his abilities on to Rogue, using her to power his machine in order to turn a delegation of world leaders meeting at nearby Ellis Island into mutants.

The X-Men move to engage Magneto on Liberty Island. After battling through his henchmen, they reach the top of the Statue of Liberty, where as a team they defeat Magneto, destroy his machine and save Rogue. Later, Xavier visits Magneto, who has now been incarcerated in a plastic prison. As Xavier concludes the visit, Magneto warns him, 'The war is still coming, Charles, and I intend to fight it.'

Trivia: Scottish actor Dougray Scott was originally cast as Wolverine, but had to pull out of the role at the last minute when filming on *Mission: Impossible II* went over schedule, leaving Hugh Jackman to win the part.

George Buza, the actor who plays the trucker who gives Rogue a lift to Alaska, also provided the voice for Beast in the early 1990s *X-Men* animated series.

The many writers who worked on *X-Men*'s 26 drafts include John Logan (*Gladiator*), Christopher McQuarrie (*The Usual Suspects*), James Schamus (*Hulk*) and Joss Whedon (*Buffy the Vampire Slayer*). Whedon would later write the first 24 issues of the *Astonishing X-Men* comic, with story elements he introduced, such as the mutant cure, incorporated into *X-Men: The Last Stand*.

What the critics said: 'It's not as good as *Superman II* and certainly nowhere near as good as the comic book; but it's good enough to raise hopes for the sequel – Marvel may yet beat DC on screen.' Joss Arroyo, *Sight and Sound*

'Singer's trump card is Hugh Jackman's Wolverine. Deeply unimpressed and permanently grouchy, the new recruit to Xavier's superhero team is the perfect guide to the *X-Men* universe.' Colin Kennedy, *Empire*

Superhero Archetype: The X-Men, though a team of super-heroes, still individually conform to the tenets of the superhero archetype. One of the most recurrent aspects of the superhero archetype across the X-Men team and trilogy of films is the dual relationship between the heroes and their mirror/antithetical villains. From the events in *X-Men*, we learn that Xavier and Magneto were once allies, and in the opening of *X-Men: The Last Stand* we see them recruiting mutants together. As former friends, both agree that there is an enmity between mutants and humans, yet how they choose to respond to this sets them apart. This archetypal trait of the mirror villain is articulated in the film by the casting of comparable actors in the dual roles. Both Patrick Stewart and Ian McKellen come from similar backgrounds geographically (both are English) and professionally (both have spent years with the Royal Shakespeare Company), and thus complement each other in the roles of the hero Xavier and his mirror Magneto. This form of casting to type was again seen in *X-Men: The Last Stand*, where the footballer-turned-actor Vinnie Jones played Xavier's antithetical villain, Juggernaut. In the comics, Juggernaut, an imbecilic, unstoppable wall of muscle, is Xavier's stepbrother, to whom Xavier stands, or rather sits, in juxtaposition – his frail, wheelchair-bound frame belying a mind the equal of his brother's brute force. Vinnie Jones's thuggish thes-pian is the perfect counter to Stewart's refined acting, neatly encapsulating the relationship between the hero and his antithet-ical villain.

Xavier is not the only X-Man to share a duality with the villain he faces. Wolverine contends with a number of mirror villains, with his feral nature reflected in *X-Men* by Sabertooth's bestial form, while, in *X2*, Deathstrike also has adamantium-laced claws as a result of government experimentation, echoing the hero's past. Throughout the *X-Men* trilogy, it is perhaps Iceman who is given the clearest mirror villain in Pyro. Both are element-wielding mutants, classmates in the first film, but, by the second chapter, Pyro's decision to leave Xavier and join Magneto places him in opposition to Iceman. The result of this decision sees the former friends locked in bitter conflict throughout *X-Men: The Last Stand*, culminating in the two letting loose the full force of their elemental powers in the film's climactic battle. Appearing to have the upper hand, Pyro mocks Iceman, telling him, 'You should have stayed in school,' but Iceman, accessing the full extent of his power, eventually wins, responding, 'You never should have left' – proving that even high-powered mutants can benefit from a good education.

Verdict: Today, with even the most obscure of heroes (*The League of Extraordinary Gentlemen* and *Ghost Rider*) now committed to celluloid, it is hard to imagine a time when *X-Men*'s big-screen prospects seemed uncertain. Yet in 2000, like the nascent creatures described in Patrick Stewart's opening evolution lecture, the X-Men fought for cinematic life. Though the comic had been a consistent top-seller since the 1980s, the characters had little exposure beyond the narrow confines of the comic-book fraternity. An early 1990s cartoon had helped boost the X-Men's profile, but the mutants had nowhere near the marquee value of Spider-Man, the Hulk or even the Fantastic Four. Also, with only one successful independent film (*The Usual Suspects*) and one disappointing studio picture (*Apt Pupil*) under his belt, Bryan Singer didn't seem the likely choice to direct. Undaunted, Singer, short on time and even shorter on money, quickly went about condensing comic histories, changing costumes and casting little-known actors, all under the scrutiny of a pedantic fanbase who were quick to find fault. The end result, with its realistic handling and character fidelity, won legions of non-comic-book fans, surprising everyone, not least the movie studios' heads, who quickly set about green-lighting anything in tights and a cape, precipitating the current superhero-movie boom.

Viewed today, the film's story may seem slight and its action sequences modest, but this allows the characters to come to the fore. A cast of then relatively unknown actors avoided any super-star pandering and equally shared the story's responsibilities. While Wolverine may have got the best lines, there was still plenty of time for Anna Paquin's emotionally fragile Rogue, the development of a love triangle between Cyclops, Jean and Wolverine, and for Patrick Stewart's Professor Xavier and Ian McKellen's Magneto to masticate superhero patter as if it were written by the Bard himself. The actors may not all have fit the look of their four-colour counterparts – a 6'2", handsome Australian playing the 5'3", feral Canuck – but they perfectly fit their roles, with Jackman's performance as Wolverine an unsurprising star-making turn.

That the strength of the characters would form the basis of a successful franchise and a new age of superhero movies is a testament to Singer's deft direction and uniformly fine actors. Later X-Men films would provide the Zip!, Bang! and Pow!, but it is this solid original that led the way.

Pow!Pow!Pow!Pow!

The League of Extraordinary Gentlemen (2003)

Cast: Sean Connery (Allan Quatermain), Naseeruddin Shah (Captain Nemo), Peta Wilson (Mina Harker), Tony Curran (The Invisible Man), Stuart Townsend (Dorian Gray), Shane West (Tom Sawyer), Jason Fleming (Dr Jekyll/Mr Hyde), Richard Roxburgh (M/Fantom/Professor James Moriarty)

Crew: Stephen Norrington (Director), James Robinson (Screenplay), Dan Laustsen (Director of Photography), Paul Rubell (Editor), Trevor Jones (Score)

Created by: Alan Moore and Kevin O'Neill

Plot: The year is 1899 and tensions are running high between England and Germany as the mysterious Fantom uses high-tech machinery to attack both countries, with each nation blaming the other. In response, aging hunter Allan Quatermain is reluctantly enlisted into the League of Extraordinary Gentlemen, a secret society brought together to protect Britain. The League has been summoned by M, and its members include the scientist Captain Nemo, the petty criminal Skinner (also known as the Invisible Man) and the vampire Wilhelmina Harker.

While recruiting their next member, the immortal Dorian Gray, the League is attacked by the Fantom's forces. Among the attackers is Tom Sawyer, an undercover American secret-service agent, who aids the League in their fight and afterwards, with Gray, joins them. In Paris, Quatermain captures the final member of the League, Mr Hyde, the monstrous alter-ego of Dr Jekyll, who agrees to join the League in return for amnesty for past crimes. Onboard Nemo's submarine, the *Nautilus*, the League makes its way to Venice where the Fantom plans to attack a conference of world leaders. Though the League saves the city, the Fantom, who is revealed to be M, escapes.

Soon after, Gray, who has been working with M, makes his getaway in a mini-submarine. He leaves a recording for the League in which he and M explain that the League was a ruse; M had wanted to get the League together so that Gray, whom he is blackmailing with his portrait, could steal Nemo's scientific inventions, Jekyll's potion, Skinner's skin sample and Harker's blood, in order to create his own super-powered armies. But Skinner is hiding onboard Gray's submarine and communicates the villains' coordinates to the League. The heroes attacks M's compound where he is manufacturing weapons to sell to the world's warring nations. Nemo and Hyde save the captive scientists; Harker battles Gray, eventually killing him by unveiling his portrait; while Skinner uses bombs to destroy the compound. Quatermain faces down M, who is in fact Professor James Moriarty. Moriarty delivers a fatal blow to Quatermain, but Sawyer manages to shoot him, with a Quatermain-inspired, long-range shot. The League brings Quatermain's body home to Africa before agreeing to continue aboard Nemo's *Nautilus*. As they walk away, the African soil above Quatermain's grave begins to stir.

Trivia: Nemo's first mate introduces himself by saying, 'Call me Ishmael.' This is the first line of *Moby Dick*. Herman Melville's book was written during the same period as the other literary works which inspired the *The League of Extraordinary Gentlemen*, and it is therefore fitting that Ishmael would appear in both the original comic and film.

The introduction of Tom Sawyer, though at odds with Moore's original comic, is not as incongruous with the character's literary history as one would expect. This character is based on a lesser-known Mark Twain novel, *Tom Sawyer, Detective*, in which the grown-up Sawyer attempts to solve a murder mystery. Originally, *The League of Extraordinary Gentlemen* contained a scene where Sawyer explained that he was hunting the Fantom because he killed his friend and partner Huckleberry Finn.

What the critics said: 'Stephen (*Blade*) Norrington's version of *LXG* is hamstrung by unnecessary changes and an incoherence that's painfully at odds with Moore's storytelling acumen.' Robert Abele, *Total Film*

'*League* might attract the under-25 crowd... But these MDCC-CXCIX-Men are no X-Men.' Kirk Honeycutt, *Hollywood Reporter*

Superhero Archetype: Throughout the Industrial Age, the unprecedented marvels and technological advances of the time were rivalled only by the writers, whose creative output drew inspiration from their promise. Visionary storytellers such as Verne, Doyle and Wells employed limitless imagination in creating wholly original characters whose influence has not diminished in the hundred or so years since they first saw print. The legacy of these Victorian heroes and villains can be seen in many of today's superheroes: before Batman, Sherlock Holmes held the accolade of 'The World's Greatest Detective'; Bruce Banner was not the first doctor with a monstrous alter-ego to Hyde; and Dracula spent his nights drinking blood long before Blade ever had fangs.

These characters may have been permitted entry to the League of Extraordinary Gentlemen by comic-book creator Alan Moore, but it was the magic of the public domain that paid their fare. With their copyrights long lapsed, Moore was free to pick and choose the characters he felt best fitted the story, and as the creator of the Manchester United of superhero teams, Watchmen, Moore knows how to fill a squad of adventurers – opting for a team that worked cohesively rather than one with the biggest stars, hence no Sherlock Holmes or Dracula. Though these characters may have had superhuman and heroic moments, and are the antecedents of modern superheroes, they are not themselves superheroes, and do not follow superhero conventions and archetypes, something Moore respected in his original work.

The film, however, takes Moore's concept and tries to shoehorn these characters into a more conventional superhero movie. But being the bastard offspring of nineteenth-century literature and Moore's fevered imagination, none of these characters fit this mould. Despite such cinematic amendments as Mr Hyde and the Invisible Man's inexplicable willingness to turn good, Mina Harker's newfound vampyric superpowers, and the villain's confounding array of secret identities, these characters do not convincingly wear this superhero drag. A sequel may have seen these characters grow into the superhero archetypes which the film sets out, but given Sean Connery's retirement and its poor box office and critical reception, we are unlikely to see these anachronistic heroes any time soon.

Verdict: In the late nineteenth century, prolific authors Arthur Conan Doyle, HG Wells, Jules Verne and their contemporaries created enduring literary icons, the superheroes of their day. The idea of putting all these characters in a superhero comic was so blindingly obvious it took a genius like Alan Moore to see it. Moore filled the ranks of his League of Extraordinary Gentlemen with aging heroes Allan Quatermain, Captain Nemo and Mina Harker and classic villains Mr Hyde and the Invisible Man. However, he was not content to rest on his main characters' literary clout, painstakingly populating his world with the most incidental characters from this literary epoch – thus Dickensian characters would rub shoulders with Captain Ahab's shipmates, and the denizens of Toad Hall were now the freakish experiments of Dr Moreau. The resulting comic, brimming with invention and wit, accentuated their human frailties in a manner that was both respectful to their literary sources and gave them renewed spark.

The superhero movie *The League of Extraordinary Gentlemen* takes the comic's premise and little else. The film begins by cleaning off the fantastic filth Moore applied to these literary inventions in order to make them presentable in a family-friendly film. Along with this sanitisation, the film also attempts to broaden the League's appeal by lowering the average age through the inclusion of the eternally young Dorian Gray, soliciting the US vote with former American icon, now gun-toting spy Tom Sawyer, and providing more obvious thrills with Mina Harker – in the comic a woman with a scar, now a bloodthirsty vampire. These uninspired revisions ensured that the characters bore little resemblance to Moore's original comic or their literary sources.

Trying to recast these extraordinary gentlemen as Victorian *X-Men*, the film winds up leagues apart from that mutant mash-up or its own source material. Stephen Norrington, who previously directed the lean superhero movie *Blade*, now produces a cumbersome action film that fails to realise its potential. The story is unnecessarily convoluted, with the villain going through three identity changes; the visuals are inconsistent, with excellent production design mired by shoddy special effects; and the principal cast fail to spark off each other. Of these extraordinary men, it is the new inclusions that fare best, with Townsend infusing the erudite Gray with superior swagger, and Shane West bringing some much-needed excitement as 'token' American, Sawyer. But Hyde and the Invisible Man are interesting visual ideas that are squandered and Nemo is given little to do except act as the League's ferryman. However, of all the missed opportunities, Sean Connery in his last pre-retirement role seems the greatest waste. As the aging hunter, the former martini shaker seems like ideal casting, but, ill-serviced by a gutless script, he fails to stir any excitement in an all-too-ordinary final performance.

While *The League of Extraordinary Gentlemen* won't go to the bottom of the superhero-movie league (that place is reserved for *Batman & Robin* and *Catwoman*), it warrants mid-table obscurity for wasting its excellent source material, legendary leading man and 110 minutes of the audience's time.

POW!

Wonder Women

'Leave the saving of the world to the men? I don't think so,' were Elastigirl's defiant first words in the animated superhero movie *The Incredibles*. But for the longest time, the ladies of superhero stories did just that, with 'heroines' such as Lois Lane and Vicki Vale usually left tied to the train tracks as the centrepiece of some supervillain's scheme. Even when superheroes made it to the movies, and Lois and Vale gained contemporary feminist sass, they were still little more than MacGuffins in mini-skirts. In the late 1970s, Wonder Woman did something to assuage the superhero gender bias on television, but the lyrics of her theme song, 'the world's waiting for you', proved prophetic, as audiences are still waiting for this satin suffragette to reach the cinema screen. In 1984, Superman's cousin Supergirl did appear in a spin-off loosely tied to the legitimate series through a shared surname and incidental characters, but while the trailer pronounced, 'Adventure runs in the family', on the evidence of the film it appears confined to the Y chromosome.

In 1992, however, two women made a mark for these heroes in high heels. The first was Buffy the Vampire Slayer; though Joss Whedon's sharp spin on the airhead cheerleader who was no villain's prey (an antecedent to *Heroes'* supercheerleader Claire), was dulled by the inanity of its big-screen realisation. The film would provide the germ for the television series that followed, with Whedon's show still the best example of a female superhero in any media outside of comics. Also in 1992, Batman got all flush under his cowl for Catwoman, his female rival in *Batman Returns*, who was not only the most interesting character of that film but of the entire series. Being neither fish nor fowl, Michelle Pfeiffer's

Catwoman was an anti-hero who saved women from being attacked but berated them for their over-reliance on a (Bat)man. Though a cat has nine lives, this particular feline would have been better stopping at one, as the risible 2004 superhero movie *Catwoman* would undo much of this earlier cat's good work.

Catwoman isn't the only modern female superhero movie that failed to reach the heights of its male counterparts. *My Super Ex-Girlfriend* unsuccessfully paired the romantic comedy and superhero movie, with Uma Thurman's superhero G-Girl's particular kryptonite being female neurosis and a dangerous inability to get over a relationship. On the basis of *Elektra*, Daredevil's previously deceased girlfriend may have been better off dead.

Lending credence to the claim that co-ed environments produce better results, the few 'super' women that have succeeded on screen are usually part of superhero teams. In *Fantastic Four* and *The Incredibles* it is Messrs Fantastic and Incredible's better halves, the Invisible Woman and Elastigirl, who save them from the clutches of their arch-nemeses; while the women of *X-Men*, Jean Grey and Storm, have long been the equals of their male colleagues. Even when it comes to villains, the *X-Men* films have proven to be an equal-opportunities employer; from Mystique and Lady Deathstrike to the all-powerful Phoenix – one of their own on a bad-hair day – the mutants have encountered more strangely dressed and potentially dangerous women than on a hen-night pub crawl.

So with successful superheroines in superhero movies, why are their solo efforts so poor? In general, the central performances are strong. Even Halle Berry seemed more comfortable in her cat skin than she ever did as the *X-Men*'s Storm. But the filmmakers treat them as a whole other species, rather than just a different gender, with the suffix of 'ine' to superhero prompting a moviemaking crisis of confidence. For instance, Catwoman may have been a take-no-prisoners anti-hero in *Batman Returns*, but in her own film she is laden with an 'Ugly Betty'-style secret identity, a whiney voiceover and an arch-nemesis who is a corrupt cosmetics manufacturer. This patronising portrayal, which has Catwoman contend with killer cosmetics while her male contemporaries are out saving the world, is as stereotypical as having a male hero don his mask to prevent a tainted batch of beer from hitting the streets. Heroes such as the working mom Elastigirl and the career-minded X-Women have shown that these characters can be superheroes whilst also retaining their femininity.

Presumably, such softening of these superheroes is meant to appeal to women, who, studios assume, only watch romantic comedies, failing to consider how the audiences for films such as *Spider-Man*, *Superman Returns* and *Batman Begins* were equally divided across both genders. In trying to pander to some elusive demographic these films patronise anyone, male or female, who has the misfortune to see them.

Some attempts have been made, however, to bring more rounded superheroines to the small screen. *Birds of Prey*, a sister series to *Smallville* featuring secondary female characters from the Batman universe may have been cancelled after only 13 episodes, but the inclusion of strong females in *Heroes* and a new Supergirl to *Smallville* have proven more successful. Nonetheless, superhero movies showcasing women have been met with resistance, as the creator of Buffy, Joss Whedon, was forced to abandon his long-gestating Wonder Woman, citing that old chestnut 'creative differences'. The character will now join the rank and file of the upcoming *Justice League of America* film. The failure of Wonder Woman looks likely to see this gender bias continue. Despite superhero movies that continue to make audiences believe a man can fly, we have yet to see a woman soar.

Buffy the Vampire Slayer (1992)

Cast: Kristy Swanson (Buffy), Luke Perry (Oliver Pike), Donald Sutherland (Merrick), Paul Reubens (Amilyn), Rutger Hauer (Lothos), David Arquette (Benny), Hilary Swank (Kimberly)

Crew: Fran Rubel Kuzui (Director), Joss Whedon (Writer), James Hayman (Director of Photography), Jill Savitt and Camilla Toniolo (Co-Editors), Carter Burwell (Score)

Created by: Joss Whedon

Plot: Living in LA, Buffy is a popular and vacuous high-school cheerleader who spends her days at the mall. However, at night, she is haunted by dreams of a vampire leader Lothos, and the young women, Slayers, who have failed to stop him throughout history. Recently, Buffy's community has suffered a spate of strange deaths, with bite marks found on the necks of the deceased, while Buffy has been followed by a mysterious man. One night, Buffy and her equally self-obsessed friends come across a pair of slackers, Pike and Benny; though each group makes fun of the other, there is a noticeable flirtation between Pike and Buffy. On their way home, a drunken Pike and Benny are attacked by a vampire, Amilyn. Though Benny is taken, Pike is saved by Merrick, the man who has been following Buffy.

The next day, Merrick introduces himself to Buffy and asks her to come with him to a graveyard so that she may discover her birthright. Though hesitant, Buffy is persuaded to go by Merrick's knowledge of the dreams that trouble her. At the grave-yard, two vampires arise from the graves of the previously dead townspeople. Using innate strength and abilities, Buffy kills the vampires. Merrick eventually convinces Buffy that she is the slayer – the next in a long line of women destined to keep vampire forces from preying on humanity. As Buffy's Watcher, Merrick trains her to slay vampires so that she will be ready to face Lothos. Meanwhile, after a visit from the now vampyric Benny, Pike decides to leave town but is attacked en route by Amilyn and a horde of vampires. Buffy comes to Pike's rescue and, as the pair go to find Merrick, they encounter Lothos, who plans to feed on Buffy. Merrick arrives in time to stop Lothos, but is himself killed in the process.

Following Merrick's death, Buffy tries to return to her former life but finds she has little in common with her old routine. As she half-heartedly prepares for a school dance, Pike sharpens every piece of available wood for the inevitable fight against the vampires. Pike arrives at Buffy's dance just as her alienation from

116

her old friends reaches its limit and the couple share their first kiss. But Pike is not the only gate-crasher, as Lothos and his vampires also arrive. Buffy takes the weapons Pike has prepared and, using a combination of Merrick's training and her own style, defeats Amilyn and the other vampires, before slaying Lothos on the dance floor. Her destiny fulfilled, Buffy hops on the back of Pike's bike, leaving her shocked, but still breathing, classmates behind.

Trivia: *Buffy the Vampire Slayer* contains early performances from Hilary Swank and David Arquette, while future superhero Ben Affleck makes a blink-and-you'll-miss-it appearance as a basketball player.

Whedon has stated that the character of Kitty Pryde, the strong-willed teen from the *X-Men* comics, has been a particular influence on Buffy. When Whedon began writing the *Astonishing X-Men* comic in 2004, he reintroduced Kitty Pryde as a prominent member of the X-Men for the first time in years.

The final film, *Buffy the Vampire Slayer*, was much lighter in tone than Joss Whedon's original script, which included changes such as Merrick committing suicide to avoid being turned into a vampire and Buffy burning down the school gym in order to kill the vampires. The television series was a continuation of the unproduced script rather than the film, and, as such, the burning down of the gym is often referenced in the series.

What the critics said: 'Cluttered with B-list names, it's full of dated pop music, silly wisecracking vampires and slapstick horror with one-note characters and senseless plotting, but Whedon's distinctive ear for teen-speak is already in evidence.' Emma Cochrane, *Empire*

'Fran Rubel Kuzui's frenzied mistrust of her material is almost total. Somebody should have given her a garlic necklace and told her to chill out.' *Time*

Superhero Archetype: With no suit, subterranean lair or catchy pseudonym, some may question Buffy's superhero credentials. Yet she fits a superhero archetype as firmly as any caped wonder. Buffy's origin meets the two archetypal events of power and responsibility; the former is the birthright she tries to ignore, the latter she gains under the tutelage of Watcher Merrick, whose death provides the traumatic event typical of a superhero's origin.

An argument could be made that Buffy does not have a secret identity. However, the way in which Buffy the cheerleader is dismissed as a vacuous mallrat, rather than the slayer who keeps the bloodthirsty demons at bay, makes her pom-poms a more effective disguise than simply removing your glasses before taking flight. Also Buffy, like all good heroes, is locked in battle with the villains who define her heroic identity. Without a fang-toothed foe to stake, she is just Buffy the high-school student, but in the midst of an undead invasion she becomes Buffy the Vampire Slayer.

She might not wear a superhero costume (it is probably a fashion *faux pas*), but by maintaining the superhero archetype beneath her risqué fashion choices and impenetrable Valley-speak, Buffy is at her core a superhero. This is one cheerleader who does not need saving, as she will save the world.

Verdict: *Buffy the Vampire Slayer* is a ludicrous mess of genre clichés, inconsistent characterisation and badly delivered dialogue. Following such a statement, one should hasten to add this is Buffy the superhero movie, not Buffy the excellent television series of the late 1990s. Though both were written by superhero enthusiast Joss Whedon, he only retained control of the series, while the earlier film was taken out of his hands and laden with a then voguish, early-1990s naffness that made it look dated by the time it reached VHS.

But beneath its sub-*Beverly Hills 90210* plotting and production are the bones of the superhero movie that would make the series so successful. Buffy begins as a pom-pom-shaking Valley girl, three fashion trends before *Clueless*'s Cher and practically a generation before *Heroes'* Claire, but when her slayer birthright makes itself known in the form of Donald Sutherland's Watcher Merrick, training montages ensue and she becomes a plainclothes superhero, born to slay. Swanson, as the titular teen, works hard in the role, looking competent as the slayer and gamely managing the stupefying Valley-speak. But where Sarah Michelle Gellar would retain the vulnerability in the hero and the hero's resolve in the girl, Swanson flits too easily between these two poles, maintaining little consistency in her performance. Of the older cast members, Rutger Hauer, perhaps taking his cues from Béla Lugosi, tries to play Lothos as a vampire lothario but comes off as a fang-toothed leech; while Sutherland seems to be counting the moments until his character's inevitable demise. Fittingly for a film that plays like a blood-sucking episode of *90210*, it is Luke Perry who fares best. As Pike, Perry walks a confident line between humour and action with slacker swagger. His is perhaps the film's only performance that would not look out of place in the series.

The film suffers most in its assumption that, by being a teen comedy first, it can get by with weak action, no narrative tension, and the production values and aesthetics of an early 1990s music video. As the mallrat gives way to the slayer, some Whedonesque moments do occur, but the film has no real bite and would be forgotten today if not for the series it produced. However, the big-screen Buffy should also be remembered for being the first non-comic-book-adapted female superhero movie. Lightly touching on issues of feminism and adolescence that would become the cornerstone of the series, this was one of the first superhero movies with a female hero who would be no one's damsel in a dress.

POW!POW!

Batman Returns (1992)

Cast: Michael Keaton (Batman/Bruce Wayne), Danny DeVito (Penguin/Oswald Cobblepot), Michelle Pfeiffer (Catwoman/

Selina Kyle), Christopher Walken (Max Shreck), Michael Gough (Alfred Pennyworth), Pat Hingle (Commissioner Gordon)

Crew: Tim Burton (Director), Sam Hamm (Story), Daniel Waters (Story/Screenplay), Stefan Czapsky (Director of Photography), Bob Badami and Chris Lebenzon (Co-Editors), Danny Elfman (Score)

Created by: Bob Kane and Bill Finger

Plot: A cry is heard from an opulent mansion as the wife of one of Gotham's elite gives birth to their firstborn son. But the newborn is disfigured, and the bluebloods celebrate their first family Christmas by taking their child for a stroll, before dropping him in the sewers along with the rest of the city's waste.

Thirty-three years later and Gotham City is again celebrating Christmas, as business tycoon Max Shreck gives a speech at the tree-lighting ceremony; but the festivities are cut short when the Red Triangle Circus Gang attack. Though Batman comes to the city's rescue, Shreck is taken to the sewers to meet the gang's leader, the Penguin. The Penguin blackmails Shreck into promising him the respect of high society, which the corrupt businessman plans to achieve by making the Penguin mayor. Meanwhile, Selina Kyle, Shreck's put-upon secretary, is again staying late at the office. But when Shreck finds Selina going through his encrypted files, he throws her from the office window. As Selina's body lies lifeless on the snow-covered pavement, a group of stray cats begin to huddle around reviving her. Returning home, a purposeful Selina creates a new identity: Catwoman.

The Penguin begins his mayoral campaign on the back of the chaos his Circus Gang creates. At the same time, Catwoman begins a campaign of her own, destroying Shreck's businesses at night while working for him as Selina by day. A more confident Selina even begins a relationship with Bruce Wayne, but the pair is constantly interrupted by their nocturnal vigilantism with Batman impeding Catwoman's vendetta. Catwoman decides to team up with the Penguin in order to discredit Batman. But the Penguin's plan backfires when Batman plays a recording of him ranting about the 'stinking city' for Gotham's citizens. The people quickly turn against the Penguin and he flees to the sewers.

Meanwhile, Selina and Bruce attend Shreck's masquerade party, during which the pair discover each other's dual identities. Suddenly the Penguin attacks, taking Shreck to the sewers. Batman foils a plot by the Penguin to kidnap Gotham's children, but the villain escalates his plans by sending rocket-strapped penguins out into the city. But Batman succeeds in redirecting this march of the penguins back to the Penguin's lair beneath an abandoned zoo. There, the Penguin and Batman struggle, with the foul villain falling to his death just as the rockets ignite, bringing down the lair. As Shreck attempts to escape, Catwoman appears. Though Batman tries to reason with her, she exacts her revenge, electrocuting Shreck. Unable to find Selina, Batman leaves just as the penguins give their former master a burial in the sewer waters. On Christmas Day, as Bruce is travelling the snow-strewn city streets, a familiar feline stalks the cityscape above.

Trivia: The corrupt businessman Max Shreck, played by Christopher Walken, is named after the silent movie actor who played cinema's first ever vampire in *Nosferatu* (1922).

Annette Bening was originally cast as Catwoman but was replaced by Pfeiffer when she became pregnant.

The part of the Penguin's father was offered to Burgess Meredith, who memorably played the Penguin in the 1960s television series. But Meredith was unable to take the role due to ill health. Paul Reubens, famous for portraying Pee Wee Herman on television, and in the Tim Burton-directed *Pee-Wee's Big Adventure*, eventually filled the role.

What the critics said: 'Though her lusty licking of Batman's face may arouse kinky thoughts, Catwoman is no bimbo in black leather. Pfeiffer gives the feminist avenger a tough core of intelligence and wit; she's a classic dazzler.' Peter Travers, *Rolling Stone*

'Where Burton's ideas end and those of his collaborators begin is impossible to know, but the result is a seamless, utterly consistent universe full of nasty notions about societal deterioration, greed and other base impulses.' Todd McCarthy, *Variety*

Superhero Archetype: Though the Catwoman of *Batman Returns* may not be the cat burglar of the comics, she does manage to steal the movie from under the men's pointed noses. Despite saving women from being attacked and having an arch-nemesis (Max Shreck) who is a bloodthirsty businessman, Catwoman is considered by many to be a villain. But just as there's more than one way to skin a cat, there's more than one path to being a hero. Catwoman is out for self-satisfying revenge and is willing to kill Shreck to get it. It is maybe this eagerness to take lives that brands her a villain. The lesser value she places on human life stems, perhaps, from having nine of her own, or living in the world of *Batman Returns* – a hyper-violent place where even the Batman kills. But it's most likely that this once mousy secretary feels, as Shreck murdered her first, that it's her turn to take the lead in their deadly game of cat and mouse.

As a vengeance-driven vigilante, Catwoman joins the ranks of the anti-hero, which includes the Crow, Punisher and Batman himself. These heroes are infected by a need for revenge with vigilantism proving a short-term cure – Catwoman's particular placebo is taking on any man who gets in her way. That the actions of these vigilantes benefit law-abiding citizens could be considered a side effect of this 'cure', rather than the selfless purpose of their deeds. Batman may better mask his motives, and his actions are therefore perceived as valiant, but there is only a whisker between the goals of the heroic Bat and the villainous Cat.

Verdict: With the Joker becoming a proverbial punchline at the end of the original film, Tim Burton moved down the pecking order of Batman's rogues gallery for the sequel *Batman Returns* to the Dark Knight's next-most-famous foes: the Penguin and Catwoman. As in the first film, Batman remains in the shadows, with the two villains (three if you count Christopher Walken's Max Shreck) hogging most of the limelight. Though the Penguin is treated as the hero's arch-nemesis, it is Catwoman who proves to be the film's most dominant character, occupying a nebulous moral position between Batman's pointy-eared justice and the Penguin's unabashed evil. It is easy to see how these 'freaks', the Penguin and Catwoman, proved to be more interesting to Burton. With their inner traumas etched on their ghoulish faces, these characters have more in common with previous Burton creations Beetlejuice and Edward Scissorhands than Batman, who, as the Penguin points out, only dresses like a freak.

In addition to these more bizarre villains, *Batman Returns* would include much of Burton's hallmark style that was absent in the pulpier original. Before Burton's stop-motion favourite, *Batman Returns* was the filmmaker's original nightmare before Christmas, with its yuletide setting providing an ironic contrast to the actions of these fractured freaks; the Gotham of the film now resembling the inside of a snow globe, its oppressive baroque architecture blanketed in white. The script, this time from *Heathers* scribe Daniel Waters, is also much better, providing plenty of room for the villains to play, and some excellent dry lines that give the kitten her claws.

To imagine these animal-themed foes, Burton applied his own scissorhands to the comic-book source material. The once-refined villain the Penguin is now a sewer-dwelling baby killer, while Selina Kyle, in the comics a tough-as-nails cat burglar, is now a meek secretary resurrected as a militant feminist with an appetite for revenge. Batman, too, strays from the comic-book code that admonishes him never to kill, willingly murdering the Penguin's most insignificant minions, making his condemnation of Catwoman's revenge reek of hypocrisy.

On the performance front, Danny DeVito makes a suitably

grotesque Penguin, but the character, despite his enduring popularity, has never easily fitted into Batman's darker stories and, despite Burton's changes, he is more of a sideshow freak than a worthy foe. A more interesting adversary is the original character Max Shreck, a snake-like corporate tycoon given venomous bite through Walken's trademark staccato rhythms. Reclaiming the mantle of the Bat, Keaton returns with his fractured hero from the original, but with less screentime the character has little space to grow. Yet all these men lie dormant in the feline vixen's thrall, with Pfeiffer quite literally the cat's pyjamas. Vamping it up with an Eartha Kitt purr, Pfeiffer digs her claws into the film from her very first whipcrack and does not let go until her closing rooftop coda. The one-time Pink Lady excels at the character's PVC-clad physicality while her bipolar fits make Keaton's Batman seem the picture of mental health. Fittingly, in a film that is as much a gothic fairytale as it is a superhero movie, it is this wicked witch who steals the show.

Pow!Pow!Pow!Pow!

Supernatural Superheroes

Although the powered protagonists of superhero movies are all 'super', few could be considered supernatural. Buffy may slay the undead, the Hulk is a monster, and more than one superhero has been resurrected, but the supernatural superheroes are rare cursed souls. As *Hellboy*'s Professor Bruttenholm explains, 'There are things that go bump in the night... and we are the ones who bump back.'

In 1954, 'eminent' psychiatrist Dr Fredric Wertham published *Seduction of the Innocent*, where he linked comics generally, and horror comics specifically, to the rise in juvenile delinquency in America following World War II. This book, coupled with the convening of a Senate subcommittee, prompted the comics industry to establish a Wertham-inspired, self-censorship body, the Comics Code Authority (CCA), which, among its many stringent and ludicrous policies, included a virtual ban on terms such as 'vampire', 'zombie' and 'terror'. The implementation of this sanitisation, which saw only comics carrying the Code's stamp of approval distributed through mainstream outlets, spelled the end not only for the horror genre, but also popular crime and romance comics, leaving the then languishing superhero genre to rise to the fore.

However, horror and the supernatural were not dead, and by the 1970s comics began to negotiate the supernatural back into the soul of the superhero, with characters like the original superhero vampire slayer Blade, Marvel's very own Hell's Angel Ghost Rider, and talking vegetable Swamp Thing becoming popular. As the restrictions on comics relaxed, more horrific monsters began to haunt comic-shop shelves. Towards the end of the 1980s, a

Swamp Thing spin-off following the exploits of blond-haired Liverpudlian magician John Constantine, *Hellblazer*, and resurrected vigilante *The Crow* reached readers, to be quickly followed in the early 1990s by the devil's own *Hellboy* and *Spawn*.

Cinema audiences, though not always receptive to superhero movies, have consistently enjoyed a good scare. So while brightly coloured, masked wonders were finding it difficult to Biff! Zap! and Pow! their way into cinemas, supernatural superheroes Swamp Thing, The Crow, Spawn and Blade, hiding under the cloak of the horror movie, managed to haunt the silver screen. Since the superhero-movie boom, even more hell-sent heroes, including Hellboy, Constantine and Ghost Rider, have arisen from their comic-book crypts to creep into the movie-biz. While these superhero movies vary as much in their quality as they do in their comic-book fidelity, with *Spawn* and *Ghost Rider* horrifying for all the wrong reasons, they are united by a central trait that defines their protagonists as supernatural superheroes.

Today, with every new superhero movie promising to be darker than the last, it has become cliché to say a superhero is 'cursed'. But the titular terrors of these supernatural superhero movies are a group haunted by Faustian pacts (Spawn, Ghost Rider), painful resurrections (The Crow, Constantine), monstrous visages (Hellboy) and inhuman blood (Blade). Each of these cursed characters is on a quest to undo the horror done unto them and to regain some sense of peace. What sets these supernaturals apart from cinema's other damned souls is that when faced with the choice of relinquishing their burden – whether it is Blade gaining a cure for his vampirism, or Mephistopheles offering Ghost Rider Johnny Blaze a way out of their pact – they choose to keep their curse and use it against the evil that spawned them, and, in enduring their torment and making this sacrifice, these supernaturals become superheroes.

The Crow (1994)

Cast: Brandon Lee (Eric Draven), Ernie Hudson (Sergeant Albrecht), Michael Wincott (Top Dollar), Rochelle Davis (Sarah),

Ling Bai (Myca), Sofia Shinas (Shelly Webster), David Patrick Kelly (T-Bird)

Crew: Alex Proyas (Director), David J Schow and John Shirley (Screenplay), Dariusz Wolski (Director of Photography), Dov Hoenig and M Scott Smith (Co-Editors), Graeme Revell and Trent Reznor (Score)

Created by: James O'Barr

Plot: On Devil's Night (the night before Halloween), police are investigating the scene of a brutal attack on a couple, Eric Draven and Shelly Webster, who were due to be wed the following evening. Eric is dead, and his fiancée dies in hospital soon after. The investigating officer, Albrecht, has to deliver the bad news to the couple's surrogate daughter Sarah. One year later, a supernatural crow returns Eric's soul to his body so he may seek justice on Shelly's attackers. Once resurrected, Eric claws his way out of his grave. Confused and consumed by anger, he applies gothic facepaint before seeking his vengeance.

His resurrected body impervious to harm and constantly guided by the crow, Eric begins to kill the members of the gang who ended his and Shelly's lives. Over the course of the night Eric is reunited first with Officer Albrecht, and later with Sarah, who is now living with her drug-addicted mother. Reaching into Albrecht's memories, Eric learns of Shelly's painful last hours in the hospital before she died. While seeking his revenge on one of the gang, Funboy, Eric meets Sarah's mother Darla. He manages to squeeze the poisonous heroin from her veins before reminding her of her duty to Sarah. Darla wakes the next morning with a fresh perspective and begins to repair her fractured relationship with her daughter. Eric, following the last gang member, Skank, finds himself at the home of the city's criminal kingpin, Top Dollar. Battling through Top Dollar's minions and associates, Eric manages to kill Skank, exacting his revenge.

Top Dollar's sister Myca realises the crow is Eric's link to the afterlife and that by killing the crow they will be able to hurt him. His vengeance complete, Eric tries to return to his grave, but Top Dollar kidnaps Sarah and takes her to an abandoned cathedral. Eric moves to rescue her but, upon arriving, the crow is shot and Eric, now mortal, is wounded. Officer Albrecht arrives to help Eric and kills Top Dollar's henchman Range, while the crow blinds Myca, causing her to fall to her death. Eric reaches Top Dollar on the cathedral roof where, following a fight, he manages to pass the pain of Shelly's last hours to Top Dollar. Overwhelmed, Top Dollar falls from the roof to his death. With Sarah safe and his vendetta complete, Eric returns to his grave as the crow flies into the sky.

Trivia: The creator of the comic book, James O'Barr, cameos in the film as a guy stealing a television from the pawnshop after Eric blows it up.

The original superhero movie *The Crow* spawned three sequels subtitled *City of Angels* (1996), featuring Iggy Pop, *Salvation* (2000), starring Kirsten Dunst, and *Wicked Prayer* (2005), starring Edward Furlong and David Boreanaz, as well as a TV series *The Crow: Stairway to Heaven*, all of which have had only minor success.

According to comic-book creator James O'Barr, one producer suggested making the film as a musical with Michael Jackson in the title role.

What the critics said: 'Unlike Schumacher with the Batman franchise, Proyas preserves that adolescent angsty feel and avoids campness at all costs. Style over content, sure, but what style.' Adam Smith, *Empire*

'It is a stunning work of visual style – the best version of a comic-book universe I've seen – and Brandon Lee clearly demonstrates in it that he might have become an action star, had he lived.' Roger Ebert, *Chicago Sun-Times*

Superhero Archetype: *The Crow* is an anomaly among supernatural superheroes in that the quest for revenge on which Eric's resurrection is predicated remains the protagonist's only goal. While other equally haunted heroes such as Ghost Rider or Constantine will stop to help those outside their vengeful remit, Eric has complete tunnel vision, confining his supernatural powers to the avengement and protection of his nearest and dearest: killing Shelly's attackers and saving Sarah from Top Dollar. But this does not make Eric less heroic; the details of how he was awarded his second life are never fully explained; perhaps stopping to play the Good Samaritan would infringe on his deal with the crow, rendering it null and void. He is also confined by a narrow timeframe that requires him to be back in his grave by Halloween. Often at the end of a supernatural superhero movie the hero will choose to keep their curse, and use it against others who would prey on the innocent, as is the case in *Ghost Rider* and *Blade*. The Crow television series *Stairway to Heaven* does posit the possibility of Eric as a Batman-like vigilante, stalking the cityscape to prevent crimes, but, based on the quality of the show, perhaps the Eric of this film is better off dead.

Verdict: Written and drawn by James O' Barr after his fiancée was killed by a drunk driver, *The Crow* was a comic that began in tragedy, while its adaptation proved to be a production that would end in one. When an on-set accident claimed Brandon Lee's life eight days before the film's completion, Lee would join James Dean and River Phoenix (and now Heath Ledger) in the ranks of promising young actors to die before their time. Watching *The Crow*, like watching Dean in *Rebel Without a Cause* or Phoenix in *Stand by Me*, it is impossible for the viewer to separate the real-life tragedy from the cinematic triumph.

Yet *The Crow* remains a success not only for its star, but for director Alex Proyas. Proyas realised the world of *The Crow* with a unified style of gothic architecture and ghoulish faces, in a cityscape drenched by a rain that bleached the colour from the screen; the original Sin City. Cloaked in the supernatural, the film is at its core a revenge narrative, its opening launching straight into the crime that needs to be avenged. While this brutal attack is never far from the hero's mind, the film does not indulge in this moment of violence, but instead uses it to propel Eric to the next part in his increasingly elaborate act of revenge. The action sequences are well handled, maintaining a level of humour and realism almost throughout, with only the film's climactic cathedral-top swordfight going a step too far.

Lee's avenging angel Eric Draven, resembling a cross between The Cure frontman Robert Smith and Edward Scissorhands, moves like a silent assassin, with Lee providing both the pathos and athleticism needed to bring the character to life. Alongside Lee, Ernie Hudson gives good support as decent cop Albrecht, while Michael Wincott plays the kind of amoral villain that has been his bread and butter since *Robin Hood: Prince of Thieves*. In the end, Proyas created a haunting supernatural superhero movie that won over those who watched out of morbid curiosity, inspiring dire spin-offs and countless teen-goth imitators.

Pow!Pow!Pow!

Blade (1998)

Cast: Wesley Snipes (Blade), Stephen Dorff (Deacon Frost), N'Bushe Wright (Dr Karen Jenson), Kris Kristofferson (Abraham Whistler), Donal Logue (Quinn), Udo Kier (Vampire Elder Dragonetti), Sanaa Lathan (Vanessa Brooks)

Crew: Stephen Norrington (Director), David S Goyer (Writer), Theo Van de Sande (Director of Photography), Paul Rubell (Editor), Mark Isham (Score)

Created by: Marv Wolfman and Gene Colan

Plot: The year is 1967 and a pregnant woman with a bloody bite mark on her neck is hurriedly wheeled into a hospital emergency room. Just as the woman flatlines, her child is born. In the present day, a young man is led by a mysterious woman to an underground club. Soon blood begins to drip from the ceiling's sprinklers as the terrified man realises the other clubbers are vampires. Just in time, Blade arrives. Dressed in black and sporting an arsenal of vampire-slaying weapons, he begins to kill any of the vampire ravers brave enough to attack him. One vampire, Quinn, though burned to a crisp, survives Blade's attack. Once Quinn wakes in a hospital, he attacks haematologist Dr Karen Jensen. Blade arrives too late to catch Quinn but takes the bitten doctor to his base of operations, an abandoned factory that he shares with Whistler, his weapons provider and surrogate father.

Whistler administers garlic to Karen to prevent her from turning into a vampire. Karen decides to help Blade in his war against vampires, including his current enemy, Deacon Frost. Frost is a rebellious yuppie vampire who has systematically taken over the upper echelons of the vampire community. During this time Karen discovers that Blade's birth to a vampire-bitten mother has given him a vampire's strength but none of their weaknesses, and that he now uses a serum to suppress his bloodlust. She endeavours to find a cure for Blade and arms him with weapons, including a blood thinner EDTA that causes vampire blood to explode.

Meanwhile, Frost attacks Blade's base while he is out on patrol. When Blade returns, he finds Karen has been kidnapped and Whistler near death. Before taking Blade's gun and ending his own life, Whistler tells Blade that Frost is planning on raising a blood god La Magra, and that Blade's blood is vital to the ritual. Blade attacks Frost's compound, where he finds a female vampire resting in Frost's bedroom. The woman is revealed to be Blade's mother, who became a vampire following his birth, with Frost the vampire who sired her. Frost takes advantage of Blade's moment of disbelief to attack, knocking him unconscious. Blade is brought to a ritual chamber where his blood drips down to the chamber's centre for a waiting Frost. In the meantime, Karen manages to escape and frees Blade, who kills the vampire that his mother has become and attacks Frost's minions, but not before

Frost can complete the ritual and become La Magra. Imbued with the power of a god, and too strong to defeat by force, Frost is stopped only when Blade injects him with EDTA, causing his body to explode in bloody eruptions. With Frost vanquished, Blade's war against vampires next takes him to Moscow, where once again Blade must draw his sword.

Trivia: An alternative ending to *Blade*, found on the DVD special features, sees Blade and Karen emerging from the subterranean ritual chamber at dawn, with the pair being watched from a rooftop by a mysterious figure. The character was to be revealed in the sequel as Morbius. Morbius was Marvel Comics' first attempt to reintroduce vampires to comics following the establishment of the CCA; the character was a vampire of scientific origins, and therefore neatly avoided censorship.

Blade is one of the few superhero movies to spawn a live-action, spin-off television series. Though now cancelled, *Blade: The Series* ran for 12 episodes with Kirk Jones playing the eponymous slayer. Other superhero movies to produce series include *RoboCop*, *The Crow: Stairway to Heaven* and *Buffy the Vampire Slayer*.

David S Goyer not only wrote all three Blade films, but produced the spin-off television series and directed the trilogy-closer *Blade: Trinity*. Goyer's first comic-book adaptation would be the ill-fated *Nick Fury: Agent of Shield* television pilot. Since stepping out from the shadow of the vampire, Goyer has co-written *Batman Begins* and is attached to direct *X-Men* spin-off *Magneto*.

What the critics said: '*Blade* is one of those all-style, no-substance, goth-mix adaptations that looks like *The Crow*, sounds like *Spawn*, and feels like *Dark City*.' Naomi Ryerson, *Mr Showbiz*

'Wesley Snipes isn't so much cast in the title role of a comic-book superhero vampire as he is infected by it. As Blade, Snipes's performance is fever-hot and artery-deep.' Michael O'Sullivan, *Washington Post*

Superhero Archetype: With few exceptions, the superhero archetype is dependent on the role of the teacher/helper, a character who provides the main marvel with power, training and/or advice. But it is not only the hero who has come to rely upon this sage-like secondary character for guidance, with the superhero-movie audience also depending on these men behind the supermen to fill in the story's often cavernous gaps. In *Blade*, the monosyllabic protagonist cannot be relied upon to relate his background for the uninitiated viewer, and so this task falls to his crotchety mentor Whistler.

Through Kris Kristofferson's rustic tone, Whistler manages to condense the hero's 35-year comic backstory for those who did not spend their childhoods following the slayer's exploits across the pages of *Tomb of Dracula*. But Whistler is shown little gratitude for this narrative cut-and-paste, as, soon after fulfilling his expositional duties, he, like many of his contemporaries (see: *Hellboy*'s Prof Bruttenholm and *Buffy the Vampire Slayer*'s Merrick), becomes expendable and is unceremoniously killed, presumably to prevent his doddering presence slackening the film's pace before the climactic showdown. However, the reports of Whistler's demise prove to be exaggerated, with the character resurrected twice more to fill in the widening cracks of the sequels' increasingly fractured narratives.

Verdict: In 1997, the rubber nipples and day-glo excess of *Batman & Robin* ensured that no one was taking superheroes seriously. However, by the end of the decade, 'respectable' superhero movies staged a comeback. While *X-Men* and *Spider-Man* would eventually win the bout, it was *Blade* that drew first blood.

The film offered a stoic, monosyllabic gothic hero at a time when vampire hunters came in the svelte form of TV's wise-cracking teen *Buffy the Vampire Slayer*. Making full use of Wesley

Snipes' athleticism and underlying gruffness, the role provided the recently troubled actor with his best screen performance, a success he is unlikely to surpass given his career's recent straight-to-DVD nosedive. Also, unlike Buffy, Blade does not have an extended surrogate family, only the crotchety Whistler in charge of weapons manufacture and narrative exposition, a role to which Kris Kristofferson effectively applies his world-weary, melancholic charm. On villain duty, Stephen Dorff balances charm and revulsion, providing strong support as vampire yuppie Deacon Frost. Yet *Blade*, unlike its sequels, remains the hero's film.

As a consequence of this hero-centrism, long tracts of the film occur where little happens and less is said, with Blade patrolling a desolate, paper-strewn city. However, when Blade is in full flight, the action sequences play out in a crimson-soaked, balletic splendour that has often been copied (see: *Constantine*, *Underworld*), but never bettered. In particular, the opening sequence in which Blade dispatches a nightclub full of vampire ravers is enough to ensure the character's superhero credentials. In 1998, Blade, a C-list character from Marvel's back catalogue, managed the seemingly impossible, bringing fresh blood to the ailing superhero movie, precipitating the genre's current good health.

POW!POW!POW!

Hellboy (2004)

Cast: Ron Perlman (Hellboy), John Hurt (Professor Trevor 'Broom' Bruttenholm), Selma Blair (Liz Sherman), Rupert Evans (John Myers), Karel Roden (Grigori Rasputin), Jeffrey Tambor (Tom Manning), Doug Jones and David Hyde Pierce (Abe Sapien)

Crew: Guillermo del Toro (Director/ Story/Screenplay), Peter Briggs (Story), Guillermo Navarro (Director of Photography), Peter Amundson (Editor), Marco Beltrami (Score)

Created by: Mike Mignola

Plot: Towards the end of World War II, a desperate Hitler looks to the occult for salvation from his inevitable defeat. On an island off the coast of Scotland, Russian mystic Grigori Rasputin, along with a contingent of Nazi scientists and soldiers, including Hitler's top assassin, the undead Kroenen, is preparing for a ritual. Professor Bruttenholm, paranormal adviser to President Roosevelt, engages the Nazis with a platoon of US forces, just as Rasputin opens a portal to Hell. The soldiers manage to destroy the portal, trapping Rasputin inside, but not before something can come through. The Hell-sent refugee is revealed to be a red demon; but only a child. He is christened Hellboy by the grunts, with Bruttenholm taking him into his care.

Today Hellboy is an urban myth, working for the Bruttenholm-run Bureau of Paranormal Research and Defence (BPRD) alongside the telepathic amphibian Abe Sapien. Though Bruttenholm is now an old man, Hellboy has aged more slowly. While on the surface Hellboy appears a large, hulking demon with red skin and a right arm made from stone (known as the 'Right Hand of Doom'), he is merely an insecure adolescent, self-consciously filing down his horns to appear more normal, and pining for his unrequited love and former team-mate, firestarter Liz.

On what starts out as a routine mission, Hellboy is called to the scene of a break-in at the Machen Library. There, he fights a demon known as Sammael, eventually destroying it in the city's subway. But using his telepathy, Abe discovers the demon was brought to life by the resurrected Rasputin and that it has laid eggs in the city's sewer. Hellboy takes a team to the sewers to eradicate the infestation. While there, the team encounter Kroenen, but, despite taking him hostage, most BPRD officers are killed and Abe is badly wounded. Back at the BPRD, Kroenen comes to life and kills Bruttenholm. After the funeral for Hellboy's surrogate father, bureaucrat Tom Manning takes control of the BPRD.

The team, now including Liz, who has suffered a dangerous relapse of her pyrokinesis, locate Rasputin's base at a mausoleum outside of Moscow, Russia. They are split up in Rasputin's subterranean lair, with Hellboy and Manning taking on Kroenen, giving Hellboy the chance to deliver a definitive final blow to his father's killer. Meanwhile Liz, accessing the full extent of her pyrokinetic abilities, destroys the last of the Sammael eggs. But in the wake of Liz's inferno, the team are captured by Rasputin, who threatens Liz's soul, forcing Hellboy to use the Right Hand of Doom to open the gates to Hell. But at the last moment, reminded of his father's teachings, Hellboy stops and kills Rasputin. On his death, Rasputin gives way to a large, tentacled demon. After being swallowed by the demon, Hellboy destroys it from the inside by igniting a grenade belt. Walking out from the scorched remains of the beast, Hellboy kisses Liz as the pair is enveloped in her blue flame.

Trivia: Doug Jones, in addition to portraying Abe Sapien in *Hellboy*, was the guy-in-the-suit for a number of creatures in del Toro's *Pan's Labyrinth*, including the eponymous faun. Jones would also play the Silver Surfer in *4: Rise of the Silver Surfer* with the character's voice provided by Laurence Fishburne.

Hellboy was renamed 'Heckboy' on some movie-theatre marquees across America's bible-belt because the film was released at the same time as *The Passion of the Christ*, and conservative theatre owners were worried that the dark and bloodthirsty film would be negatively impacted upon by del Toro's heartfelt comic caper.

The voice of Abe Sapien in *Hellboy* was provided, uncredited, by David Hyde Pierce. Pierce was joined in the superhero pantheon by his *Frasier* co-star Kelsey Grammer, who in 2006 filled out the fur of Beast in *X-Men: The Last Stand*. Eddie the dog could have made it a hat-trick of heroes for the Crane boys, but was narrowly beaten to the role of *Underdog*.

What the critics said: 'Now that the comic superhero film has largely replaced the monster feature, *Hellboy* happily combines the two.' Rob Mackie, *The Guardian*

'*Hellboy* succeeds because it brings the visuals from the page to life with a beating red heart.' Kim Newman, *Sight and Sound*

Superhero Archetype: Despite being a relatively new hero, Hellboy's origin has an age-old familiarity. Arriving on Earth as an orphan from a distant world, Hellboy was taught by a caring adoptive parent to use his otherworldly powers to fight for the American Way; now who does that remind you of? There are more than a few similarities between the Big Red One and the Blue Boy Scout.

Like Superman, Hellboy arrived on Earth at a seemingly arbitrary point; while Superman crash-landed on Earth amongst the wheat fields of Kansas, Hellboy arrived like a bat out of Hell on a small Scottish Isle. Yet as soon as the infant Hellboy grasped a 'Baby Ruth' candy bar, offered by American Bruttenholm, in his stone-like fist, Hellboy pledged his allegiance to the Stars and Stripes. And it was lucky too, as it is hard to imagine Hellboy being found by a local and brought up the Scottish way, as a kilt-wearing demon hunter, who would only eat an American candy bar if it had been deep-fried in batter first; at least his inexplicable facial hair and ruddy complexion would not look out of place in downtown Glasgow on a Saturday night.

With both Superman and Hellboy in the service of Uncle Sam, these American immigrants try to blend in with the locals as best they can. For Superman, this is achieved by slipping on some glasses, brushing back his split curl and assuming a state of nervous disposition. No such charade can hide Hellboy's monstrous visage, and, despite taking an angle grinder to his hellish horns, Big Red is not able to walk the streets unnoticed. It is one of the hero's most noble attributes that he fights for an American dream his nightmarish appearance prevents him from enjoying. It seems, though Hellboy's powers are hell-bound, his upbringing has given him a red, white and blue responsibility.

Verdict: Fresh from directing one superhero movie, *Blade II*, Mexican director Guillermo del Toro took a little-known, gothic anti-hero and created *Hellboy*, a modest superhero movie that has inspired a dedicated fanbase to rival any in the canon. In casting his supernatural superhero, del Toro avoided the obvious Hollywood possibilities (legend has it that Vin Diesel was interested) and went instead with his *Blade II* stalwart Ron Perlman. Though normally confined to tough-guy roles in lacklustre action films, Perlman was an ideal choice for the misunderstood spawn of Satan. Attacking the role with devilish intent and emoting from under a ton of prosthetics and red make-up, he managed to convey the awkward tenderness beneath Hellboy's monstrous exterior. Hellboy was not the only character effectively brought to the screen, with the role of his surrogate father Professor Bruttenholm warmly rendered with trademark gravitas by John Hurt; while David Hyde Pierce on vocal duties and Doug Jones in costume collaborate fluidly to create the amphibian hero Abe Sapien, and Selma Blair provides the sparks as Hellboy's old flame Liz. In fact, it is this makeshift family of monsters that is the film's greatest strength, with their (in)human interactions giving the audience heroes they can really root for.

It is therefore a great disappointment that the film largely fails to offer any villains against whom our heroes can test their mettle. The evil head honcho, Grigori Rasputin, behaves more like an erudite vodka salesman than the mad monk; his glacial Nazi girlfriend has all the stagnancy her demeanour would suggest; while Rasputin's henchman is Sammael, a dividing Rastafarian demon who would not look out of place on Sesame Street. Thankfully, one excellent villain appears with nearly enough menace to redeem the whole bunch. Kroenen, a decrepit clinical killer with sand in his veins, a clockwork mechanism in his heart and blades projecting from each arm, offers the only real venom in the villains' otherwise toothless bite.

Though competent, the film's action sequences never really take advantage of our heroes' potential, as the film weakly climaxes with Rasputin transmogrifying into a 50-foot garden slug that Hellboy, no table salt to hand, easily dispatches with some orally administered grenades in yet another missed opportunity.

With a great collection of characters and a charismatic central hero, *Hellboy* is never less than enjoyable. Let's just hope the upcoming sequel's 'Golden Army' can really put the boy through Hell.

Pow!Pow!Pow!

Superbad

While this book is a celebration of superhero movies, it would be negligent not to briefly acknowledge some of the super-clunkers this genre has produced. The superhero has always aimed to be a big-screen institution, and though various external factors have until recently prohibited the realisation of this goal, the genre's greatest enemy has often been itself; with any triumphs quickly blotted from memory by pale imitators, cheap comic-book adaptations and lazy sequels. This is certainly true of the superhero movie paragon *Superman*, which had its luminous celluloid triumph dimmed by the dire *Superman III* and *Supergirl* spin-off, and all but extinguished by *Superman IV: The Quest for Peace*. With Donner's original becoming a Christmas television staple, so too have the increasingly shambolic follow-ups. This yuletide packaging has meant that the Superman films have become jumbled in the public consciousness, a veritable gag reel of classic moments from the original, undercut by crass set-ups from the sequels. The Batman franchise may also have been afflicted by declining sequel quality, but possibly a greater hindrance was the number of second-rate vigilantes that scampered across the screen following its initial success. In the early 1990s Batman's street-cred was quickly tainted by the big-screen company he kept – a group of ne'er-do-wells that included *The Phantom* (Billy Zane squeezed into a purple spandex sock) and *The Shadow* (Alec Baldwin hidden behind a crimson scarf). For the longest time Superman and Batman remained two islands of credibility in a sea poisoned with toxic films such as *Howard the Duck*, *Steel* and *The Punisher* (the 1989 Dolph Lundgren version, although the recent effort was only marginally better).

Even today, now that the superhero movie genre has shaken off its reputation for producing schlock, the successes often fail to outweigh the disappointments. 2007 will be remembered for yielding a particularly poor crop. While many were expecting *Ghost Rider* to be a shambles – and weren't disappointed, with the flaming skull looking healthier than the gaunt, too-old-for-this-shit Nicolas Cage – and the Fantastic Four did little to warrant being taken seriously in their sophomore effort, the 'safe bet' *Spider-Man 3* caught the dreaded 'curse of the three' that has ruined many a potentially classic trilogy (see: *Return of the Jedi*, *The Godfather Part III* and superhero movies *Superman III*, *Batman Forever* and *X-Men: The Last Stand*). Other recently lambasted efforts have included sorry spin-offs *Catwoman* and *Elektra*, the worn-out *Jumper* and the clearly mislabelled *The League of Extraordinary Gentlemen*.

Every genre has its missteps, but the superhero movie must tread more carefully than most. When your cast is dressed in brightly coloured costumes and using dialogue that's likely to incite laughter if badly delivered, the film can quickly descend into end-of-the-pier pantomime. With this inherent risk of falling flat on your face, the many successful films this genre has produced are superhuman achievements indeed. Yet, while audiences believe that these Supermen can fly, they have also come to expect more than a few to come crashing back down to Earth.

Batman & Robin (1997)

Cast: George Clooney (Batman/Bruce Wayne), Arnold Schwarzenegger (Mr Freeze/Dr Victor Fries), Chris O'Donnell (Robin/Dick Grayson), Uma Thurman (Poison Ivy/Dr Pamela Isley), Alicia Silverstone (Batgirl/Barbara Wilson), Michael Gough (Alfred Pennyworth)

Crew: Joel Schumacher (Director), Akiva Goldsman (Story and Screenplay), Stephen Goldblatt (Director of Photography), Mark

Stevens and Dennis Virkler (Co-Editors), Eliot Goldenthal (Score)

Created by: Bob Kane and Bill Finger

Plot: A new villain haunts Gotham as Batman and Robin make their way to the scene of a museum break-in. There Mr Freeze, a large man in a specially designed coldsuit, is stealing a giant diamond. The dynamic duo engages the villain but is eventually given the slip when a reckless Robin is caught in the ray of the villain's freeze gun. Meanwhile, in a laboratory deep in the jungle, homely scientist Pamela Isley learns that her demented boss, Dr Woodrue, has been using her research to develop 'Venom', a super-soldier serum that he plans to sell to the world's despots. Realising Isley has found out about Venom, Woodrue kills her, leaving her in a pool of chemicals on the laboratory floor. But Isley is reborn, imbued with plant-like properties and a toxin-delivering kiss of death; she is now Poison Ivy.

Batman decides to set a trap for Freeze by putting the Wayne jewels on public display. Freeze, a former scientist, takes the bait as he needs the diamonds to cure his cryogenically frozen wife, who is suffering from an advanced stage of MacGregor's Syndrome. But Ivy crashes the party, and using plant pheromones to bewitch the caped crusaders, absconds with the diamonds. Freeze, who is 'cold' to Ivy's womanly wiles, in turn steals the diamonds from her. However, intrigued by Freeze, Ivy suggests a partnership. The 'unabominable snowman' sends his new cohort to collect his comatose wife, but, threatened by any competition, Ivy pulls the plug on Freeze's wife's chamber, telling him that Batman killed her. With nothing left to live for, Freeze agrees to Ivy's plan; to first freeze Gotham, and then the world.

At Wayne Mansion, Alfred's niece Barbara has come to visit, but their joyous reunion is cut short when Alfred is taken ill with MacGregor's Syndrome. Barbara soon stumbles across the secrets of the Batcave and outfits herself with a Batsuit. This 'Batgirl' quickly comes to the rescue of the caped crusaders, who, though wearing rubber lips to avoid Poison Ivy's deadly kiss, have become entangled in her vines. The combined Batfamily defeat Ivy and quickly make their way to the Gotham Observatory, which Freeze has fitted with a telescopic cold-ray, plummeting the city into an icy grave. Batman manages to defeat the frost-bitten foe by attaching a Batheater to his suit, while Batgirl and Robin, using satellites to transfer sunlight, thaw the city. Now that Freeze is incapacitated, Batman tells him that his wife is still alive, and, upon regaining his humanity, the one-time doctor offers Batman the cure needed to save Alfred. With Alfred healthy, the dynamic duo agrees to let Batgirl join them as a trio of crime-fighters.

Trivia: Mr Freeze was elevated from the gimmicky criminal of the comics to a tragic villain in the *Batman: The Animated Series* episode *Heart of Ice*, which established the character's backstory as a scientist who froze his ailing wife in order to find a cure for her terminal condition. This plotline, but not the character's pathos, was used for *Batman & Robin*. *Heart of Ice* would receive an Emmy award and is a fan favourite; *Batman & Robin* holds no such accolades.

Dr Jason Woodrue, the wild-haired scientist who kills Uma Thurman's Pamela Isley, is played by John Glover whose other superhero credentials include Lionel Luthor, Lex's father in *Smallville*, and voicing the Riddler in *Batman: The Animated Series*.

Though demoted to a grunting henchman in *Batman & Robin*, Bane was an important character in the comics throughout the 1990s. He is particularly remembered for breaking Batman's back during the year-long story arc, *Knightfall*.

What the critics said: '*Batman & Robin* lives and dies by the aesthetic of excess, the familiar idea that anything worth doing is worth overdoing.' Kenneth Turan, *Los Angeles Times*

'Like a wounded yeti, *Batman & Robin* drags itself through icicle-heavy sets, dry-ice fog and choking jungle vines, before dying in a frozen heap.' Desson Howe, *Washington Post*

Superhero Archetype: With teen-heroes such as Spider-Man and Buffy proving that you don't need adult supervision to be a superhero, there has been little demand for sidekicks on screen. Even the greatest advocate of heroes in short-pants, Batman, operated alone until his third cinematic outing, *Batman Forever*. Perhaps Tim Burton felt Gotham's dangerous streets were no place for the Boy Wonder. In fact, even in the 'innocent' days of the 1950s, more than a few eyebrows were raised at the idea of Bruce Wayne sharing his cavernous mansion with a prepubescent, who he dressed in tights to take on nocturnal crime-fighting sprees. In his 1954 book *Seduction of the Innocent*, eminent psychiatrist and four-colour mudslinger Dr Fredric Wertham claimed Batman and Robin were 'a wish dream of two homosexuals living together'.

As the comics progressed into darker tales, the idea that Batman would endanger the life of a child snapped the premise's already well-stretched credibility, and the original Robin, Dick Grayson, was allowed to grow up and fly the nest, becoming Nightwing. However, DC Comics felt fans still wanted a sidekick for Batman and introduced Jason Todd as the new Robin. But this character's angst and impudence saw him become unpopular with fans, leading DC to cynically ask readers to decide via a phone vote whether the youngster should die following a vicious beating from the Joker. By a narrow margin of 72 votes, the Boy Wonder was no more. But of course a new teen titan would take on the mantle, with the current Robin, Tim Drake, being a popular combination of Dick Grayson's enthusiasm and contemporary attributes.

Batman & Robin sticks with the Dick Grayson version of Robin, and, from the opening close-ups of the caped crusaders' rubber-encapsulated rears, the film does little to dispel any lingering gay rumours. However, by presenting the character as a late-teen, and even swapping the green-and-red suit of *Batman Forever* for a *Nightwing*-inspired number, the film does manage to offset some of the more ridiculous elements of this crime-fighting partnership. Though Robin is unlikely to make an appearance in any future Christopher Nolan-directed Batman film, an oft-mooted *Teen Titans* movie may see this bird fly on screen again.

Verdict: 'Nana-nana-nana-nana-nana-na… Batman!' Even for the purists who get on their soapbox to deride its campy tone and comic-book infidelities, the 1960s Batman television series still represents for many their first adventure with these men in tights. It is almost impossible for Batfans of yesteryear not to get a giddy, nostalgic kick out of its mantra-like theme song, Adam West's unshakably deadpan delivery, and the many colourful, onomatopoeic sound effects that Biffed!, Zapped! and Powed! their way across the television sets of our childhood. Though harking back to this series rather than the Burton films or the comic books, it is hard to imagine that the memory of Joel Schumacher's *Batman & Robin* will evoke anything other than bile from today's young Batfans. Since its release in 1997, there has been so much scorn poured over Schumacher's craptacular caped crusader that it seems almost unfair to add another volley. But some crimes should never be forgotten, lest they be repeated (take heed *JLA* director George Miller).

So round up the usual suspects! Public enemy number one would have to be Joel Schumacher who, following on from *Batman Forever*'s mystifying box-office popularity, turned in an over-produced neon nightmare loosely resembling something a dog might throw up after ingesting too many glow-sticks and tinsel. Among the actors squeezed into this hideously designed world include the future Governator, Arnold Schwarzenegger, who received top billing. His poor judgement in accepting a role in which he looks like a perma-frosted Fester Adams while delivering one-liners of such bad quality they would look out of place in a Christmas cracker, is enough to warrant any right-thinking

Californians to demand a recall. Perhaps sensing this was merely a pit stop on his way to superstardom, George Clooney – whose Batman makes his entrance by sliding down the back of a dinosaur *à la* Fred Flintstone – spends the majority of the film hiding behind a nonchalant smirk, which disturbingly doesn't leave his face even when he delivers the grave news of Alfred's imminent demise.

Though an encounter with the plant poison ivy could be discomforting, lying in a bed of the irritating weed would be bliss next to the cringe-inducing sight of Uma Thurman trying to ooze sex appeal as she stripteases her way out of a fluffy, pink gorilla suit. After the unnecessary addition of Chris O' Donnell's Robin to the Batfamily – the actor is now given rubber lips to complement the rubber nipples and acting style he displayed in *Batman Forever* – *Batman & Robin* invites another unwelcome guest with the inclusion of Alicia Silverstone's Batgirl. Had Schumacher wielded the megaphone on another Batman (mis)adventure, Ace the Bathound and the extraterrestrial Batmite may well have joined the burgeoning crime-fighting syndicate.

The plot is so ridiculous, it is almost beyond comprehension, and even if scriptwriter Akiva Goldsman was dictated to by merchandisers and a glitter-obsessed director, there is no excusing the woeful dialogue. While the Batfilms had never been noted for tonal consistency, this superhero movie didn't see the franchise jump-the-shark, so much as vault it with a ten foot Batpole.

Though the Burton/Schumacher films had always tipped the scales in favour of the villains, the ridiculous rogues of *Batman & Robin* would eventually collapse the franchise, enabling Christopher Nolan to create a more hero-heavy series and allowing Batman finally to begin.

Pow!
(obviously)

'Nuff Said!

Traditionally, the superhero movie is one cinematic creature that struggled to maintain its place in the big-screen animal kingdom. But in 2000, *X-Men* mutated the genre, and, in a medium built on the survival of the fittest, this evolution equipped the super-hero movie with the opposable digits necessary, not only to survive on screen, but to reign triumphant. However, the genre's place at the top of the celluloid food chain has recently come under threat. Superman's return was greeted with exacerbated yawns and fanboy cries of infidelity rather than the expected fanfare. Once-vital super-franchises (*X-Men* and *Spider-Man*) have since been diluted by weak trilogy-closers; and Hollywood seems to have found some new, or rather old, toys to play with, as the bewildering success of *Transformers* prompts movie-studio execu-tives to run from the comic shop to the toy store in search of inspiration.

However, despite these recent missteps, there is little to suggest that the high-flying success of superheroes will be grounded any time soon, with more heroes donning capes and taking to the skies than ever before. In summer 2008, after the anaemic *Superman Returns*, a new Man of Steel arrives in cinemas, but this alcohol-soaked weapons manufacturer will not be on a 'Quest for Peace'; rather Robert Downey Jr's *Iron Man* will be opening a (tin)can of whupass on the silver screen. Iron Man will not be the only superhero with a weakness for the sauce this summer, with Will Smith playing an alcoholic, narcissistic superhero in need of better PR in *Hancock*. Soon after *Hancock*, Batman returns in *The Dark Knight* to play his trump card – the Joker, and Hellboy unleashes *The Golden Army* for his long-awaited sequel. The summer season also sees the return of the original Mr Incredible, as the Hulk trades Ang Lee for *Transporter 2* director Louis Leterrier, with Edward Norton filling out the purple pants. Hopefully this directorial seesaw will not reduce the Green Goliath to a mindless beast, but allow *The Incredible Hulk* to smash both on screen and at the box office.

2009 looks set to be even more prolific, with Wolverine taking a page out of Batman's book and beginning again with his own solo superhero movie. This prequel, awkwardly titled *X-Men Origins: Wolverine*, should answer such important questions as: Who gave Logan his claws? What is Weapon X? And how does Wolverine get his gravity-defying quiff? While audiences know what they can expect from this X-Man, there are two very uncertain prospects resting on the cinematic horizon. *Justice League of America* will unite the brave and the bold of DC Comics: Wonder Woman, Green Lantern, the Flash, and, in a move likely to confuse and detract from their own films, Batman and Superman. Yet rather than cast Christian Bale or Brandon Routh, director George Miller seems to be looking to the ranks of US teen soaps to fill the capes and cowls of these icons of superherodom, resulting in a roster that reads more like the Teen Titans than Justice League. A more tempting prospect is the big-screen realisation of Alan Moore's superhero masterpiece, *Watchmen*. With a cast chosen not for their voguish profiles but their acting pedigree, and in Zack Snyder a director with the successful comic-book adaptation *300* under his belt, *Watchmen*, though unlikely to achieve the genre-redefining success of its source, should still have fans counting down to its release.

Another masked marvel to look forward to in 2009 is the cinematic debut of the Spirit, legendary sequential-art innovator Will Eisner's influential comic-strip hero of the 1940s. *Will Eisner's The Spirit* will mark the solo directorial debut of prodigious comic-book writer/artist Frank Miller (*Sin City*, *300* and *The Dark Knight Returns*). Miller is one of the many talents, including Kevin Smith, Joss Whedon and forefather of the genre Richard Donner, who are now working heavily in both comics and films, marking a cross-pollination of talent between the fields, which should propel the passage of superheroes to the screen faster than a speeding bullet. With nearly every superhero going from mooted to movie in less time than it takes Joel Schumacher to ruin a franchise, some other superhero movies soon to be winging their way to the screen include human Fourth of July *Captain America* (dir. Nick Cassavetes), hammer enthusiast *Thor* (dir. Matthew Vaughan), picnic-ruiner *Ant-man* (dir. Edgar Wright) and DC Comics' resident speedster *The Flash* (dir. David Dobkin).

Since being crippled by a speculation-market crash in the mid-1990s, comics have been overtaken by cinema as the greatest proponent of all things 'super'. In many ways, the mass exodus of superheroes from the comic-book page to the silver screen is comparable to the origin of the first superhero, Superman. Like the Last Son of Krypton, superheroes have left their ailing home, comics, and come to a new one, cinema, where their native attributes – their archetypes, mythology and stories – have made them unique and consequently successful. Further mirroring the Man of Steel, the genre remains steadfast in its quest to protect cinema audiences from the twin villainy of boredom and convention, by creating imaginative stories of selfless heroes, fearless adventurers and supermen who fly through the night sky protecting the ones below. This book told the story so far, a story, like all good superhero tales, that looks set 'to be continued' for many years to come.

'Nuff Said!

Excelsior! A one-on-one with Stan Lee

From webbed wonders to green goliaths, the world of super-heroes is indebted to the tireless creative output of one man above all others, Stan Martin Lieber; better known to his comic-book friends as Stan Lee. Lee began his career in four-colour capers in 1941, aged 17, as the text filler for *Captain America # 3*, and within months he was writing his own stories. By 18, Stan was editing the entire line of Marvel Comics (known then as Timely Comics). But by the early 1960s, the stringent implications of the Comics Code Authority (CCA) pushed the industry to near collapse. Stan was considering a move to more 'legitimate' literature when his publisher Martin Goodman asked him to create a new superhero team. With what could have been his last roll of the superhero dice, Stan tried something different; he created a family of superheroes with extraordinary powers but ordinary problems. Through the *Fantastic Four*, Stan embraced the human in the superhuman, allowing superheroes to soar to greater heights than ever before. Over the next decade of unpar-alleled creativity and imagination he created, with the equally legendary artist Jack Kirby, heroes such as the Incredible Hulk, the X-Men, The Mighty Thor (with contributions from Stan's younger brother Larry Lieber), Ant-Man, Silver Surfer and the Avengers; with Steve Ditko, Spider-Man and Doctor Strange; with Bill Everett, Daredevil; and with Don Heck and Larry Lieber, Iron Man.

Stan's impact on superheroes reached beyond his canonical creations, resurrecting vintage heroes Captain America and Namor the Sub-Mariner. He also challenged the CCA with a socially engaged Spider-Man story that addressed the negative effects of drug use. The draconian code had prohibited any reference to drugs even in a cautionary tale and would not give the comic its seal of approval. Stan still ran with the story, receiving critical acclaim and forcing the CCA to redefine its crippling policies, thereby allowing more diverse and darker stories to be told within the superhero genre and beyond. Stan's success also forced Marvel's rival publisher DC Comics to take stock, with DC codifying its conflicting character portrayals and striving for greater story continuity, as used by the young upstart. Stan also fostered a sense of community among the isolated comic readers, engaging fans through letters pages, the bullpen and Stan's Soapbox, where the avuncular writer tackled the problems of the day in his trademark hyperbolic prose.

Stan Lee's influence can never be underestimated, taking on what had been a languishing genre and outfitting it with new ideas; creating indelible characters that are both modern myths and pop-culture favourites; and in the process revitalising not only a genre but a whole medium. Despite being primed for big-screen success since their inception, it would take four decades for Stan's characters to go from static to motion pictures. In 2000, *X-Men* started the evolution, followed in quick succession by *Spider-Man*, *Daredevil*, *Hulk* and *Fantastic Four* with *Iron Man* and a new Hulk film (*The Incredible Hulk*) due this summer, while *Ant-Man*, *Thor*, *Doctor Strange* and a solo *Silver Surfer* film are all in the pipeline. Today, 'Smiling' Stan Lee has a lot to be happy about, and I spoke to the man, the myth, the legend to discuss superhero movies from early struggles to recent successes.

Why is it, with so many of your characters entering the fifth decade of their publication, that it is only now these superhero movies are coming to the screen?

I think people have wanted to make movies of them way before, but the special effects weren't available. They couldn't figure out: how do you get the Human Torch to burst into flame and fly; how do you get Spider-Man swinging on his web? We had to wait until the special effects were developed to the point where they could do all those things.

Do you think it is just the technology or are there possible sociological reasons?

I think people just like these kinds of stories, you might call them high-concept stories, you know. When they were children, most people liked fairytales – tales of giants, witches, monsters and dragons – and as you get older you can't keep reading fairytales, but I think you never outgrow your love for things that are bigger than life and very colourful.

How do you feel the superhero archetype has changed in its transition from the comic-book page to the big-screen?

Well, they try to change it as little as possible, but anytime you adapt something from one medium to another, you have to change it to make it suitable for that medium. So there are little changes made sometimes in the way the character looks, and the way the character speaks, or what she or he does. But generally with the Marvel characters we've been pretty lucky, they have stayed pretty true to the way they were written and drawn in the comic books.

Which of the recent superhero movies based on your work do you feel best represents the characters and worlds you created?

Well, I think probably *Spider-Man*; I think that comes the closest.

Is Spider-Man your favourite superhero movie?

Yeah, I think so.

Do you have a preference for the first two Spider-Man films, which are more closely based on your stories, than the third, which drew on stories and characters from later books?

No, [*laughing*] I like them all equally. The only thing that could have been a little different in the third one was that I thought the Sandman was too big. I don't know why they turned him into the giant that he became. I thought it would have been more interesting if he was just a normal-sized person, but somehow it got a little too fantastic when he became so gigantic. But it was probably done because when people go to the theatre they just like to see things that will absolutely knock them out. I suppose their thinking was, 'Well, let's make him real big and that will impress everybody.'

That's similar to what they did with the Hulk.

Yeah, that's quite right.

Do you think that super-sizing the characters removes the human element?

It removes a little bit, but again it's for the big screen, for people in the theatre, and they may feel that's what they need.

Have you been surprised by the tone taken by some of the adaptations from your work?

No, not really, they weren't too surprising. I was aware that they were going to stay very close to the original concept in the comics, and I've always been very pleased by that.

Even the Ang Lee-directed *Hulk*'s more meditative approach?

Well, I thought it went a little bit too far with that business of Bruce Banner's childhood, and the evil father he had. I thought it took it away from the fun that the movie should have been.

In that case, would you prefer a more traditional adaptation, as in the Bill Bixby television series?

Absolutely! I think the next Hulk movie [*The Incredible Hulk*] may be a little closer to the way the comic books were.

Not including a superhero movie based on one of your own characters, do you have any particular favourite?

Yeah, I thought the first *Superman* was awfully good. I thought it was great, I think that'd be my favourite.

Is there much rivalry between Marvel and DC over the big-screen success of your heroes?

Well, actually we're all friends. The people at DC and the people at Marvel are very friendly – one of my best friends is Paul Levitz, who is the president of DC. There's a rivalry in the sense that we all hope our movies will do well. I also hope the DC movies do well; it's good for the whole business.

Any favourites among those not based on a comic book?

The cartoon [*The Incredibles*], that was a masterpiece, I loved it!

Of course, this developed the idea of a family of superheroes, which you introduced with the Fantastic Four.

The funny thing is, we had a show that we were about to sell to television about a funny superhero family, and when they started work on *The Incredibles*, we couldn't sell it because it was too close to theirs.

How do you feel about some of the liberties these superhero movies have taken with your characters?

Again there's a reason for that. I remember when Jim Cameron (*Titanic, The Terminator*) thought he would do the Spider-Man movie, he also felt that the web-shooting should be organic rather than through web-shooters, it's just better for the movie; like the costumes for the X-Men, it made more sense. I think they would have looked silly running around in brightly coloured uniforms. They looked more like they belonged to this day and age by getting those black, sort of leathery suits that they all wore.

As the comics and film industries become more closely aligned, do you ever wish you had made the leap to writing for film yourself?

Absolutely! I wish I had come out to Hollywood years ago, I surely do.

Would you have been interested in writing superhero and adventure stories or would you like to have explored different genres.

I like to write everything. The thing I like to write the most is humour. In fact, I have a new company called POW! Entertainment. We have a couple of humorous movies that are being developed, comedies along with some superhero things, so I like to write everything but somehow I find I enjoy writing humour the most.

With your POW! Entertainment designing superheroes directly for other media, do you think the comic industry's days are numbered?

Oh no, I think there will always be comic books. People still enjoy picking up a relatively inexpensive magazine and reading it, sharing it with a friend, rolling it up and putting it in their pocket, and collecting them. Fans like comics! [*pauses*] But obviously there are so many other things today. Years ago, when I was doing the comics, the only real competition was radio or movies. Then, after a while, television was the competition, but now you have video games, computers, iTunes and millions of other things. [*pauses*] Comic books are also a very good breeding ground for movies, so many people now do comic books just hoping a movie producer will read it and go, 'Wow, this will make a great movie,' so even the people who do comic books have their eye on Hollywood.

You have made a number of cameos in recent superhero movies. Do you have a particular favourite?

Well, I like the one I did in *Spider-Man 3*, and I liked where I was the postman in the *Fantastic Four* movie. It's hard for me to remember all of them. I have a great one in the *Iron Man* movie; wait until you see that, it's very funny.

Can you give us a hint of what we can expect?

Tony Stark walks over to me at a big party where everybody is beautifully dressed. I'm wearing a tuxedo and a smoking jacket and I'm smoking a pipe with my arms around three beautiful blondes, and he walks over to me and says, 'Hi Heff' and then 'Oh excuse me, I thought you were Hugh Heffner,' and I say, 'That's ok, I get that all the time.' It's a very funny little bit that has absolutely nothing to do with the story.

In *Fantastic Four* you played Willy Lumpkin, an actual character from the comics. Are there any other existing characters you would like to play in your future cameos?

I'd be happy to play anything, but actually the choice isn't mine, it's the director's. The director of the *Fantastic Four* (Tim Story) thought it would be good to make me Willy Lumpkin, and I said, 'Oh great,' so it's up to them; whatever it is they want me to do, I'm happy to do it.

Are there any of your superheroes that have yet to come to the screen, which you would like to see as the focus of a superhero movie?

Oh they're all coming to the screen: *Doctor Strange* is in the works; *The Avengers* is in the works; *Shield*, every one of them.

Is there anyone in particular you would like to see starring and directing?

No, the people who make those choices have made some pretty good choices. I'm happy to let them do it.

Finally, congratulations on your upcoming star on the Hollywood Walk of Fame. Do you feel you and your fellow superhero creators get the recognition you deserve from the superhero movies?

Oh, I probably get more than I deserve.

Index

POCKET ESSENTIALS **FILM** STOCK TITLES

9781903047002	Alfred Hitchcock NE Paul Duncan 4.99
9781904048602	Agatha Christie Mark Campbell 4.99
9781904048497	Andrei Tarkovsky Sean Martin 6.99
9781903047460	Animation Mark Whitehead 4.99
9781904048589	Australian Film £4.99
9781904048404	F.Scott Fitzgerald Richard Shephard 4.99
9781903047637	Film Music Paul Tonks 3.99
9781904048671	Film Noir Paul Duncan 4.99
9781904048503	Film Soleil DK Holm 4.99
9781904048435	Film Studies Andrew M Butler 4.99
9781842433010	Filming on a Microbudget NE Paul Hardy 4.99
9781842432839	French New Wave Chris Wiegand 4.99
9781904048596	Great British Movies Don Shiach 4.99
9781904048466	Hitchhikers Guide M J Simpson 4.99
9781904048558	Italian Cinema Barry Forshaw 4.99
9781842432853	Laurel & Hardy Brian J Robb 4.99
9781903047668	Martin Scorsese Paul Duncan 4.99
9781842432863	Orson Welles Martin Fitzgerald 4.99
9781904048374	The Oscars John Atkinson 4.99
9781904048367	Quentin Tarantino DK Holm 4.99
9781904048510	Robert Crumb DK Holm 4.99
9781903047446	Science Fiction Films John Costello 4.99
9781904048299	Steven Spielberg James Clarke 4.99
9781842432266	Tintin Lofficier/Lofficier 4.99
9781842432808	Vampire Films Le Blanc/Odell 4.99
9781904048312	Writing a Screenplay John Costello 4.99

Available from all good bookshops or send a cheque to: **Pocket Essentials** (Dept SS), P.O. Box 394, Harpenden, Herts, AL5 1XJ. Please make cheques payable to **'Oldcastle Books'**, add 50p for postage and packing for each book in the UK and £1 elsewhere.

Customers worldwide can order online at www.pocketessentials.com